Affirmative Aging

AFFIRMATIVE AGING

A Resource for Ministry

Edited by
Lorraine D. Chiaventone and Julie A. Armstrong
for
the Episcopal Society for Ministry on Aging

PERENNIAL LIBRARY

Harper & Row, Publishers, San Francisco
Cambridge, Hagerstown, New York, Philadelphia, Washington
London, Mexico City, São Paulo, Singapore, Sydney

Library of Congress Catalog Number: 85-51011

ISBN: 0-86683-786-8

87 88 89 90 MPC 10 9 8 7 6 5 4 3

Contents

The study programs are based on the following premises:
1. Self discovered learnings have more meaning and lasting effect than acquiring information.
2. New learnings are possible, when we share our experiences of what helps or hinders.
3. Program formats are constructed to be used by clergy and laity who may or may not have specific expertise. Leadership requirements are a spirit of openness and adventure.
4. Chapters from the book must be read before each session. Sessions can be used as a series, or as resources to explore the content of a specific chapter by a special interest group or decision making body. Sessions can also be modified to fit time boundaries.

AFFIRMATIVE AGING can be ordered through your local bookstore or directly from the ESMA office. Further resources are also available from ESMA.

Contributors

Emma Lou Benignus has studied in philosophy, theology, adult education, and gerontology, taught at university and seminary level, and written many articles. She has worked with churches in America, Europe, and Africa and has directed the national Aging Program for the American Baptist Church. Her focus now is on the spiritual growth of the elderly.

Eugene C. Bianchi, Professor of Religion at Emory University, is the author of *Aging as a Spiritual Journey* (Crossroad, 1982). In addition to conducting conferences and workshops on aging and human development, Dr. Bianchi has written a new book, *Meditations on Aging.* His other books and articles range widely over religious, cultural, and psychological issues.

Robert W. Carlson is Professor of Ministries at Seabury-Western Theological Seminary in Evanston, Illinois. Prior to his seminary teaching he served for seventeen years as rector of the Church of the Nativity, near Washington, D.C. Professor Carlson's interest in the field of aging began in parish ministry with the discovery of the rich resource of wisdom found in elderly members. He teaches a course on aging in which equal numbers of seminary students and older people meet to learn about and discuss issues of aging.

Claudia B. Cluff is Program Associate, The Third Age Center, Fordham University, and is Assistant Rector, Church of St. John the Evangelist (Episcopal), New Brunswick, N.J. From 1980 to 1982 she was Program Director, Ministry on Aging Project, Episcopal Diocese of New Jersey—a parish-based volunteer program to provide informal support to impaired elderly persons. Reverend Cluff has authored a manual for volunteer programs for the aged (*The Frail in Our*

Midst), and has published papers on issues concerning older persons.

Leighton E. Cluff is Executive Vice-President, the Robert Wood Johnson Foundation, Princeton, N.J. He has taught at the University of Florida College of Medicine and the Johns Hopkins University School of Medicine, written extensively about medical care, education, and research, and contributed to advancements in the provision of health services for aged persons in the community, nursing home, and hospital. Recently he had a pivotal role in formulating an interfaith volunteer caregiving program that supports services for impaired elderly persons in twenty-five communities nationwide. He has served as a consultant to national and international agencies and has lectured throughout the United States and abroad.

Charles J. Fahey has been director of the Third Age Center at Fordham University in New York since 1979. He presently serves as a member of the Federal Council on Aging and the Advisory Committee of the New York City Department on Aging. He was a member of the Vatican delegation to the 1982 World Assembly on Aging and of the National Advisory Council of the 1981 White House Conference on Aging. A frequent resource person for government, church, and social service groups, he has received the National Award of Honor of the American Association of Homes for the Aged.

Helen Kandel Hyman is a freelance writer and editor now living in Connecticut. Her books include *A Treasury of the World's Greatest Fairy Tales* (1972) and, with Barbara Silverstone, *You and Your Aging Parent* (1976, revised 1982). The latter was a Consumers Union Book Selection.

Frances Reynolds Johnson is coauthor of the *Study Guide for Affirmative Aging*. She authored ESMA's *Age in Action* educational materials for 1984 through 1986. Mrs. Johnson is a graduate of Union Theological Seminary and Windham House and has had extensive Christian education experience in parish and diocesan positions.

Martha Kate Miller is a free lance writer and editor, she holds an M.A. from Chicago Theological Seminary and has taught at both the University of Chicago and the University of Colorado. She has worked as an actress in professional theater and network television, has hosted numerous radio interview programs, and is a frequent lecturer.

Herbert O'Driscoll, a native of Ireland, is rector of Christ Church (Anglican) in Calgary, Alberta. He has served parishes in Ireland and Canada, been a chaplain in the Royal Canadian Navy, and been Warden of the College of Preachers at Washington Cathedral, Washington, D.C. He has spoken extensively in the United States and Canada and written hymns, radio and television scripts, and nine books.

Nancy J. Osgood is Assistant Professor of Gerontology and Sociology at Virginia Commonwealth University/Medical College of Virginia in Richmond. She is a member of the Service and Rehabilitation Committee of the State Division of the American Cancer Society. She is coordinator for the senior citizens' group at Colosse Baptist Church, West Point, Virginia. Her books include *Life After Work: Retirement, Recreation, and the Elderly* (1982); *Senior Settlers: Social Integration in Retirement Communities* (1982); *Suicide in the Elderly: A Practitioner's Guide to Diagnosis and Mental Health Intervention* (1985); and, with Patch Clark, *Seniors on Stage: The Impact of Applied Theatre on the Elderly* (1985).

Charles W. Pruitt, Jr., is President of the Presbyterian Association on Aging, a nonprofit corporation providing facilities and services for older persons in southwestern Pennsylvania. Mr. Pruitt joined the field of elderly housing and long-term care in 1965 as Executive Director of the Cathedral Foundation, Jacksonville, Florida, following positions at the University of Florida. Active in the Episcopal Society for Ministry on Aging since 1966, Mr. Pruitt currently serves as its national President.

Nancy Roth is an Episcopal priest who teaches prayer and meditation, Christian yoga, and dance prayer at Trinity Church, Wall Street, New York City, and conducts workshops and retreats throughout the United States. An experienced spiritual director, she is also Program Coordinator of Holy Cross Monastery, West Park, New York, where a popular aspect of the monastery's guest ministry is a series of Elderhostel weeks attended by over four hundred seniors each year.

Editors

Lorraine D. Chiaventone is executive director of the Episcopal Society for Ministry on Aging. As such, she administers the Episcopal Church's national program on aging, helped establish a national volunteer aging network, coproduced "The (In) Dignity of Aging" national satellite teleconference with Trinity Institute, produced "Aging is Jazzy" benefit with Jonathan Winters, and acts as a consultant to ESMA educational materials, and a managing editor of Aging Accent. She represents ESMA in national and international organizations.

Julie A. Armstrong is the program consultant of the Episcopal Society for Ministry on Aging. She has education and experience in leadership training, technical assistance, and program development. She served on the Michigan Governor's Commission on Aging and the Michigan Council of Churches Committee on Aging. Armstrong is the past chair of the Diocese of Ohio Training Division and served on the Province 5 Leadership Training staff. Armstrong was resident scholar at Trinity Parish in the City of New York representing ESMA.

Preface

The fastest growing segment of our population is those over sixty-five. We are all faced with changes brought about by a graying population. Thus the Episcopal Society for Ministry on Aging envisioned a book on spirituality in the aging process that could be a resource for both church and society.

This book's intent is not to treat the themes in a definitive way. It is rather to expand the reader's consciousness, to create awareness of the scope of issues related to aging, and to spark the imagination in meeting the challenge of new situations.

Because Christian spirituality "always has a corporate dimension," as Robert Carlson writes in his chapter, "The Gift of Wisdom," we decided that a book on spirituality and aging would not be written by one author only. Thus came the quest for authors who through their own experience and knowledge could discover, amid the inevitable losses of old age, opportunities for creative life-styles and relationships. *Affirmative Aging* lifts up longevity as a blessing and a gift, while pointing to the reality of the limitations experienced in the aging process. With spirituality as a common basic undergirding, the authors address the varied needs and interests of today's elderly and those who minister to them and with them.

In paying tribute to all who made this book possible, special words of praise are first reserved for the eleven authors who both gave life to our vision and displayed extreme patience through unforeseen delays in publication.

Our thanks to Avery Brooke, who, while publisher of The Seabury Press, first presented us with the vision that ESMA, as the Episcopal Church's national agency on aging, conceive and publish a resource book to raise the church's consciousness of its mission to develop a ministry on aging.

We wish to pay special thanks to our consultant, Martha Kate Miller, whose editorial skills drew forth, to borrow her own words, "our most creative thought toward developing an ecology of aging, one in which the individual is nurtured and the whole of society reaps the harvest."

ESMA acknowledges the guiding hand of Hermann Weinlick, Winston Press editor and liaison person. We also extend a note of thanks to those who read manuscripts critically and offered various suggestions to improve the book.

Finally, our sincere thanks as editors to Mary Ann Gordon, ESMA secretary, our Board of Directors and its Officers, Provincial Coordinators and Diocesan Designees, and other friends who encouraged and supported us through our memorable journey in the publication of ESMA's first book.

Lorraine D. Chiaventone and
Julie A. Armstrong,
Editors,
for the Episcopal Society for Ministry on Aging

Aging, a Spiritual Journey
T. Herbert O'Driscoll

If we are honest, all writing about aging is autobiographical, for either we are already aware of our aging or we anticipate it with as infinite a variety of responses as we bring to anything else. In recent decades the succession of our years has become the stuff of much thought, investigation, questioning, and statistical study. The reasons are obvious. We are living longer, a statement only slightly shadowed by the "we" being an actuarial calculation rather than a personal guarantee. Inexorably the mean age of our society is moving higher and higher. The practical consequences of this trend may be readily seen. The more subtle effects, such as newly emerging leisure patterns, changes in pace, tone, and priorities of thinking, will become evident more gradually. There will be marked effects on art, literature, and all other products of human imagination. If wisdom really is a gift of old age, we are perhaps bound for a more philosophical civilization. A darker thought is the possibility that passivity, another companion of advancing years, will pervade society at levels both physical and mental.

While we can learn much from projections and statistics and calculations, we are still humbled in our efforts to foresee the quality and texture of a future in which the human life span will be significantly lengthened. We Westerners are patently gifted in matters of technology

1

and the production of material goods. Our capacities for enriching the human experience and steering a safe course on the inner journey are less certain. It is to considerations relating to the *quality* of one's advancing years, then, that this book is oriented. It is not merely one more book in the mounting tide of books about aging. It specifically stakes out a territory within that process, the territory we have called spirituality.

The moment I see that last sentence I realize how very much of the twentieth century and of Western civilization it is. It makes two assumptions which seem self-evident to us, but would be incomprehensible to earlier ages. One assumption is that human experience is sectional and that one such section is a "thing" called spirituality. The other is the assumption that there is something more inclusive or universal of which spirituality is only a part. What aspect of human experience is outside the province of the spiritual? Are there actually elements in human experience not spiritual? We have only to ask the questions to realize how much the Christian in us clashes with the acculturated twentieth-century citizen.

The answer to all such questions is, for a Christian, a resounding "No!" Human experience is unthinkable without its also being a spiritual experience from birth to death and beyond. In the life of any particular individual there may be no institutional form of spirituality, no church envelopes on the writing desk, no familiar hymns learned or credal statements formed. But we are as much spiritual beings as we are sexual beings. To be human is to be spiritual.

2

The moment in the second chapter of Genesis (and it matters not at what level of the literal or the mythic we read it) when the Creator takes dust and breathes into it the breath of that same ultimate life which streams through the galaxies is the moment of our conception as spiritual beings. Far from being merely a part of our humanity, spirituality defines our humanity.

I shall age in the company of many spirits, welcome and unwelcome. Now halfway through my sixth decade, I sometimes detect the cloying presence of a spirit of self-pity, sometimes a spirit of fear, frequently a spirit of anxiety. All can at this stage be repulsed by activity, involvement, creativity, but I am under no illusion that these diversions will forever be available as allies against the invasion of those dark shadows of my being. Which spirit will be the richest and closest companion of my senior years? I do not yet know. I know what my hope is: that I may encounter one who offers new creation in exchange for my diminishing powers, bright visions for my failing sight, and intimations of resurrection for my expectations of death.

You will have noticed that I have moved from the general to the particular, from the plural to the personal. I do so for a reason. I observe that many who write about the things of our human aging adopt an objective stance. I am quite sure that frequently it is an unconscious protection against associating the self with the subject of aging. We have endless devices for this sort of thing. We reflect philosophically about aging by reaching through time and culture for jewels of wisdom dropped by the great. We offer data about an exterior and abstract thing called "aging," statistics involving white-haired legions

3

who march in some comfortably distant decade. We use distancing language, words such as "they" and "the aged." It is said that Damien, priest on Molokai, truly became a minister to his leprous congregation the day he began his sermon to them with the words, "We lepers. . . ." We need not address our aging as a terrible disease (though much in our culture does just that), but as an aspect of human experience that will best be reflected upon by men and women who do not seek to deny its reality for themselves.

Allow, then, some personal reflection. I shall be fifty-six years old by the time these thoughts see print. From the vantage point of someone twenty or twenty-five years older, that age may be regarded as inadequate for the purposes of this book! But I am aware of certain realities. Whatever my state of health, there are changes taking place in my body, changes in appearance, in energy levels, in appetites. I am aware that within a decade I must arrive at what is still official retirement age. Within the last month I have received news of the deaths of two of my university contemporaries. I am aware, too, of other changes. Because they are taking place in my inmost being, they are more difficult to express. But the fact is that the patterns of my spirituality are changing.

I am a child of the church from birth. Growing up in the south of Ireland in the 1930s meant that I grew up in a world where Christian faith was utterly universal, where the sacredness of the natural world and the reality of the spiritual world were strongly present. Neither Enlightenment nor Industrial Revolution had yet demolished the sacred ladder set up between earth and heaven. I can recall no moment of "becoming a Christian." Flashes of awareness of the presence of God, of "epiphany," of "annunciation," have come often. In such moments, faith is realized and nourished. God comes near, Christ encounters us, our searching soul glimpses a Shining City. But like all visions, these moments are given and taken, they are found and lost and must daily be sought again, for those are the terms of our earthly relationship with the Kingdom of Heaven that surrounds us.

This process I find becoming richer in recent years. There are hints appearing in things I write, clues in my homilies and meditations. I say they are "appearing." Why do I write of it in this way? Because it is not a change I have intentionally sought. I have encountered a reality beyond myself, an "other" meeting me on my journey, a reality that first came toward me from beyond, but now walks with me and indeed has entered more and more into my being.

What is this "it"? I know, yet I shall never fully know. It is that mystery that touched me in my baptism, while I was still all unknowing of it. It has engaged my attention a thousand times in the years between, greeting my partial vision in unnumbered disguises: in the beauty of nature, in dreams, in the ecstasy of love, in the subtlety of relationships, in sacrament, in the warmth of community, in moments of solitude, in the instant of creativity.

I know that this "it" is more than an "it"; for, mystery though it be, it invades my personhood and therefore must itself be personal, must have being and identity and name. I speak, as you well know, of the Holy Spirit.

5

I cannot remember a time when there was not in some sense a realization of this presence, yet I am aware of it more richly in recent years. I am aware, too, of a wish to be more intentional about the exercise of this sense of presence. I have felt grateful for the moments given, for the glimpse of doorways opening on hidden levels of being. Yet I realize now that I have been a receiver rather than a discoverer. Now I wish to seek out this presence, rather than presume there will always be unexpected encounters. I find that in my reading there is less searching for more information or practical insights for ministry or parish administration. Rather, I want to explore the vast and lovely country of rich spirituality that bears the footprints and echoes with the voices of those who have experienced both the presence and absence of God as they lived out the journey I myself must pursue.

My generation has undergone many changes in its understanding of the Christian faith. The years immediately following World War II saw a "boom" in church life and organization. In a twilight decade of consensus about national objectives and social mores, the institutions of church and society in the 1950s and early 1960s saw themselves as working together for worthwhile, if rarely defined, ends.

Then came a revolution that changed and is still changing every facet of our lives. A severe questioning of all traditional values took place. Old loyalties were no longer taken for granted. Many left organized religion to follow their own quest in their own way. Hungry for spiritual food and drink, many in the 1970s turned to the East for nourishment. Many traditional practices such as yoga, genuine and therapeutic in themselves, flowed into Western life. Eastern spiritual leadership was sought and followed.

While reasons for this attraction varied, the nearest thing to a common factor was a rejection of Western activism and a longing for elements felt to be absent from the Christian tradition, at least from the Christianity of recent centuries. Among these elements were meditation, contemplation, and a sense of intimate relationship with the earth.

All this has not made recent Christian experience either comfortable or easy. Within the Christian community itself vast and deep change has had to be experienced. Sensibilities have sometimes been grievously hurt. Many have known great agony of mind and spirit. But out of this cauldron of intergenerational experience has come a new church and a new spirituality. Perhaps we should say there has come a newly vitalized church and spirituality, for much that is central to the life of faith today is ancient treasure rediscovered.

Christians of all ages are discovering the flow of energy that comes from a faith stance that is consciously chosen rather than merely inherited and therefore sometimes taken for granted. They are coming to a deeper appreciation of the sacred meal of the Christian community that we call Eucharist. They are realizing the powerful way in which it can gather a People as they journey through a wilderness of change and threat. They are realizing that however fine and dignified our formal religion may have been, there may also have been an aspect of shallowness. There is in many a sense of moving into something deeper and richer. External things, things

7

learned cerebrally, are yielding their single dominance to include more richly the internal, the experienced, the intuited. We are recovering a sense of mind and heart informing us equally. Christian religion has rediscovered Christian spirituality. Religious system is enriched by spiritual journey. Faith is being more and more understood not merely as a body of knowledge we do or do not believe but also as a mystery which can give meaning to our experience and become a resource for our daily living.

At the heart of all this, a revitalized liturgy proclaims the central and indispensable truth for this or for any other generation of Christians.

Christ has died.
Christ is risen.
Christ will come again.

That short exclamation sings that human life is not merely a journeying away from a youthful innocent awareness of Christ as Lord and friend toward a sad and wiser adulthood beyond such naivete. We possess a Christ who is the resource for this hour and for all that lies ahead. He is Lord of the past, the present, and the future. Our years are a life-long pilgrimage towards him.

Much more follows from that realization. The central events of Christian faith take place not only in the past but within the ongoing experience of our daily lives. Bethlehem and Calvary and the Garden Tomb are not merely places in a long ago time or a faraway geography. Daily within each of us something of God seeks to come to birth. Each of us is potentially a Bethlehem. When I wrong or betray or hurt others, there is a sense in which I crucify them. In like fashion, I am myself subjected to

8

little crucifixions. In such ways each of us can become a Calvary. But then the mystery we know as resurrection can also take place within each of us. We can recover from crushing defeat. We can transform destructive attitudes. Faith can overcome doubt, despair give way to joy. In such experiences we possess in ourselves the transforming power of resurrection.

Within the last ten years Christian faith has shown an immensely creative response to the spiritual hunger felt by a whole searching Western culture. We have realized the extent to which Western culture, affected by such events as the Enlightenment and the Industrial Revolution, allowed the meditative and contemplative experience, as well as the creation-centered aspects of Christian tradition, to be nearly forgotten by all but a few. Timeless Christian spiritualities are again nourishing us, particularly the Celtic, Franciscan, and Orthodox. Also available to us, yet for the most part spurned and misunderstood, are the deep insights of Native American spirituality, such as those of Chief Seattle. We are seeing more and more accessible translations of writings from all of these sources. We are hearing the voices that have spoken to us of such things in our own time, voices such as those of Teilhard de Chardin, E. F. Schumacher, Donald Allchin, Alan Ecclestone, Urban Holmes, and Madeleine L'Engle. All offer themselves to us as we seek spiritual resources for the future.

One other element of contemporary spirituality must be named. For a long time the Christian message was focused on personal life, its relevance seen primarily in terms of the individual. Still, there have always been those who challenged such a limited vision. Old Testament prophets inveighed against it in their day, John Wesley and Elizabeth Fry in theirs. We have heard Dorothy Day, Thomas Merton, Martin Luther King, Jr., Dietrich Bonhoeffer. These men and women, and many others, would claim that Christ is Lord not only of personal life, but also Lord and Judge of institutions—corporate, political, and, for that matter, ecclesiastical.

While many of our generation have found it difficult to understand this aspect of Christian spirituality, it has helped to create links between our faith and our daily participation in corporate and political structures. We are coming to see that we follow one who is Lord of all aspects of our experience.

I am convinced that those of us who will live out our senior years through the close of this century are the fortunate recipients of a rich inheritance of spirituality only recently recovered. To realize this can be a most valuable corrective when we are in a mood to lament the quality of our time in history and to cry with Hamlet,
The time is out of joint; O cursed spite;
That ever I was born to set it right!
You and I have seen much storm and noise of battle. We have seen our most deeply held beliefs and traditions brutally challenged. We have heard faith questioned, moral positions attacked, God dismissed as dead. To all this, you and I have been far more than spectators. By our decisions, our ideas, our energy, you and I, wittingly or not, have contributed to the totality of what is now afoot. And the world has been transformed before our eyes into a place of vast complexity, immense achievement, unprecedented danger.

In the contemporary wilderness there may be bitter waters, but there are also the sweetest and purest of deep-flowing wells. There may be hunger in our weary twentieth-century souls, but there is a spiritual bread that is fulfilling, energizing, and inexhaustible. We are pilgrims well supplied for the journey, supplied by the Lord of the city to which we go.

Deo Gratias!

Toward an Ethic
for the Third Age

Charles J. Fahey

It is estimated that at the time of Jesus only one person in ten lived to be fifty. At the beginning of this century only half the population survived to the age of fifty. Today, two-thirds of us will live into our eighties.

Like most blessings, this one comes mixed with new challenges peculiarly its own. For the fact is that neither society at large, nor the institutions that serve society, nor the individuals most concerned have ever experienced anything like it before. We're not even certain of the questions to be raised, let alone equipped with the answer.

As a species, we have a great proclivity for so objectifying challenges as to lose touch with their reality. We assess the past, project the distant future, gather statistics for today. We speak of "they" and "them" and draw learned conclusions regarding procedural policies. It makes us feel objective, in control, safe. But only the most dedicated illusionists can handle the phenomenon of widespread prolongation of life in this manner. With any luck at all, the "they" of this matter will be "we" one day. You and I. Aging is an intensely personal affair that at the same time carries implications for every aspect of our culture.

The generations alive today have been given a gift of life not only fuller in a human sense than that of any period in history but also longer. We must struggle to understand the meaning of the gift of aging and to rethink its place in the divine economy, in the life of every social institution including the family, and in the life of every individual.

Like many other social institutions, the church has tended to think of older persons only within the context of frailty and vulnerability. Indeed, it is fitting that in accord with our preferential option for the poor we have special concern for those whose poverty is exacerbated by age or infirmities. But there is more! There is a new ethical agenda to be identified. What values sustain persons in this new milieu? How will work, wealth, power, status, and resources be shared equitably? What is required to develop a just, appreciative, and compassionate consciousness in younger generations?

One way of approaching this new situation is to speak of three periods of one's life, the Three Ages of a person. The first part of life is the time to grow in the use of "head, hands, and heart," to grow "in wisdom, grace, and age." While these are lifelong activities, they are the primary task of the First Age.

The Second Age is marked by autonomy and certain fundamental choices: what I am to value and cherish, what persons and causes I am to identify with, what I am to do as work, who my friends are to be, whether I am to marry and have children, where I am to live. These choices having been made, the many other choices of one's life tend to be subordinated to the activities and sacrifices associated with maintaining them. One's status is achieved by fulfilling the roles inherent in these fundamental options.

For most people in history, death would intervene before this phase of life was completed. Even through our parents' generation, a life span that extended beyond this point was perceived as merely winding down, not as entering into another viable phase. Beyond the Second Age, one embarked upon the long, sad decline. Once the traditional role of the Elder was devaluated by modern society, status went into distinctly short supply for these graying citizens.

We're beginning to grasp the fact that significant portions of our society are living thirty, even forty years beyond the completion of the Second Age. That constitutes a definable entity we must acknowledge as the Third Age. This Third Age phenomenon is new. While there have always been old people, only now has this become the *expected lot of virtually everyone*. The ramifications of this fact reach into every aspect of our culture. There are economic, social, psychological, and political consequences, as well as profound spiritual and ethical implications.

For all too many, descent into one's "declining years" is the signal for a kind of inertia to set in, a lapse of energy and purpose that precludes a creative approach to the rest of life. But the Third Age, whether viewed within a secular or sacred context, can be a time of conscious decision making, a graceful period in which older persons may return the gifts they have received, a time to reengage with the broader society, not alone as a

14

family member and as a worker but as a citizen of the world with the heavy responsibility to give.

Older persons have a personal and collective story to tell. Not merely a narration of events, but one that is filled with reflection and value judgment. One that recognizes incongruities and paradoxes, one that elicits both rage and laughter. It is a story that may be illumined by the incomparable gifts of perspective and balance.

This generation of elders has experienced and caused more social change than any in history. This is a gifted generation. And we surely need what it has to offer. We need people who are the memories of neighborhoods and families and labor unions and churches. We need those who remember segregation and the Holocaust, Hiroshima, and a nation without Social Security and the Salk vaccine. We need people with a sense of history, a vision of the future, and a conscience.

This societal need resonates with the psychological and spiritual needs of persons in the Third Age. Among those factors that cause problems for older persons is the loss of role and status often associated with retirement. The concept of active aging can mean a restoration of both.

What roles can the church play in helping us deal with the fact of the Third Age? A preliminary analysis of data being gathered as part of Fordham University's Third Age Center studies of the church and aging indicates that churches are more likely to interact well with their older members if they do so out of a principled, deliberative commitment, rather than a hit and miss approach that is largely dependent upon the interests and skills of the primary pastoral figure.

Perhaps the most extensive and significant role of the local congregation is providing the older person with a sense of belonging and stability in a rapidly changing world. This is best done on an intergenerational basis. But in order for such an integration to take place at an optimal level, barriers both psychological and physical must be removed. As we know, painfully, the church is affected by the dominant culture. As ageism exists in the broader society, it also is found in the pews. It is all too easy for churches to consign older persons to their "place."

Even if the church is a hospitable place psychologically, it may be quite difficult from a physical point of view. Some churches are notorious for the poor quality of their sound systems; others have dangerous stairs; some have no restroom facilities. Often there is no transportation available to and from the services.

Still, sensitivities are becoming more acute, and churches are discovering more of their potential for service. Perhaps the most common of all formal services is convening older persons and facilitating opportunities for them to discern their needs and develop their own programs. Among the most popular projects to grow out of this kind of approach are nutrition programs being sponsored or hosted by neighborhood churches.

We need involvement with others at every stage of life, but particularly in the later part of life. Satisfaction with one's situation is influenced dramatically by the availability of a confidant. Parishes are acting both as "the significant other" for persons without family or friend and in support of those who fulfill this function. In the former role they serve as recruiters, brokers, trainers, and consultants for those in need and those ready to serve. Increasingly, they offer support to those who have the care of a frail person. It is estimated that for every person who is in a formal system of care, there are two others who are being cared for by family, friends, or neighbors. When asked what kind of assistance they would need if they were to care for a frail person, those who never had done so indicated that they would need money. On the other hand, those who actually have the care of such a person replied that their need is for respite, training, professional backup, and psychological support. A number of congregations run support groups and information programs for such persons.

As an aside to this discussion, a fascinating finding shows that neither money nor the availability of support is critical in the decision to care or not care for a disabled person. The most significant factor is whether people cared for one another in the past. Unless people sang, laughed, and danced together in easier days, it is unlikely that they will stand by one another in difficult times.

Among the special charisms local congregations need to encourage are flexibility and readiness to assume significant responsibility for the *whole* person. We have programs, professionals, agencies, and funding patterns for a series of diagnoses, age groups, and types of care. In the name of professionalism and accountability, the purview of professionals and their programs has continued to narrow. Yet, as people age, their needs become more complicated, and their ability to negotiate the system becomes more limited. Unfortunately, the church can fall into the same trap, and the excellent can become the enemy of the good.

When there is little intentionality about the Third Age, people tend to drift into it and through it without realizing its meaning and opportunities. The church has many approaches to education and personal development, but virtually none of them has the Third Age on the agenda, despite the fact that significant if not disproportionate numbers of our members (to say nothing of clergy and religious) are in the Third Age.

The changing demographic reality poses a series of new questions concerning the meaning of life in the Third Age, the role of family in a four-and five-generational milieu, and the just distribution of benefits and burdens, particularly through the political process. Clearly we have given insufficient thought to these matters. We need a humble but concerted effort to integrate pastoral experience, gerontological insights, and theological discipline within the context of good pedagogical technique to assist our parishioners in their spiritual pilgrimage in the Third Age.

A variety of educational approaches ranging from the pulpit to the small prayer group can enrich the lives of older people, if we are but creative enough to see the possiblities. Marriage encounter programs, for instance, have assisted many couples in their lives together, but there seems to have been little effort to utilize this tool for those who are in or near the Third Age. Unfortunately, church-related family progams have been oriented almost exclusively to parents and young children.

The failure to recognize such opportunities for ministry is significant, both in terms of human need and in sheer numbers. Many couples will spend the major part of their lives having completed their primary parenting role, a fact that is probably not unrelated to the increasing rate of divorce among Third Age couples. We need to rethink our perspectives concerning marriage, not only for older persons, as preparation for the later years, but also to further understand the purpose of marriage in the Second Age. We need to discover the reciprocal roles of husbands and wives throughout the entire span of marriage and to enhance our understanding of intimacy, sexuality, and the independent/interdependent roles of men and women who are individuals as well as couples.

Women live on average seven years longer than men. Women over sixty-five are six times more likely to live alone than are men. Surely we can devise more imaginative responses to these facts than the organization of support groups for widows. The church has an obligation to teach people of all ages and all circumstances how to marshal their own inner resources and draw sustenance from the Source of all strength. And the day of an emergency is a poor time to begin.

While congregations are disproportionately gray, few sermons are addressed to the needs of older parishioners. Intergenerational solidarity is a concept with which the church has a great deal of sympathy. But it must also develop a more sensitive response to the specific needs of its older constituents in that area in which the church has a special competency: the meaning of life and death.

Is there a unique spirituality of the Third Age? Do life experience, changing social roles and relationships, modified physiological capabilities, and approaching death have such impact that older persons have a distinct way of approaching the Lord? Are there pastoral implications in the Third Age?

Few persons have reflected on these questions, and there has been virtually no systematic approach by the church in this area, though there are some stirrings of interest in doing so. The New York State Catholic Conference has initiated a Commission on the Elderly that has identified this area as one of its priority considerations.

Timothy M. James has offered the interesting observation that while a Harris poll found that 71 percent of people over sixty-five found religion "very important" to them, compared with only 49 percent of other adults, the next most comforting feature of their lives was television. Surely one possible inference from this curious juxtaposition of facts is that when interpersonal relationships become attenuated, other "dimensions" are invoked as solace. There are strong clues for pastoral direction here.

Whether people actually become "more religious" in the latter part of their lives is unknown. Clearly some do, and just as clearly some do not. The criterion of churchgoing itself is of dubious validity as far as spirituality is concerned. Those who are in church are not necessarily religious, and those whose faith is most evolved may be prevented from church attendance by physical disability. But for many persons religion is a major source of stimulation, direction, and consolation in life. Older persons are entitled to the ministry of the church and to participation in active ministry themselves, particularly in the area of the interior life.

One of the tenets of ageism is that older persons are unable to change. The church has given way to such a mindset in failing to challenge older persons to live a more intense interior life.

Interior prayer has at least two fundamental aspects to it. It is a reaching out to God to express praise, thanksgiving, sorrow, or need. It is also an event that naturally and/or supernaturally affects the consciousness, the convictions, and the emotional and physical state of the person praying. As our understanding of the whole-person health movement within the structure of conventional medicine broadens and deepens, it becomes increasingly evident that an individual's prayer life is in no way peripheral to his or her general wellbeing.

Prayer always happens in a context. It is an event within the life experience, the present, past, and future of the person praying. In the case of the older person, there are many years of experience to color and inform the prayer life. Older persons come to the moment carrying a lot of baggage, good and bad. There are psychological patterns, styles of imaging and remembering. Available energy and physical and mental capabilities may be critical factors.

By the same token, the issues confronting each individual are different by reason of age, status, and role. In the First Age one is a "beginner" living in a circumscribed world that offers a relatively narrow range of life experiences. While feelings may be intense, the God

21

experience is limited. In the Second Age the exigencies of everyday life color one's practical knowledge of prayer. Family, work, and community make inevitable demands that cannot help but influence both the content and the style of private worship.

In the Third Age there is the opportunity to gain perspective and the time to develop the "skill" of prayer. Life is a continuum, and the present builds on the past, but past patterns do not dictate absolutely the mode of present behavior. One can teach old dogs new tricks.

In the Third Age one can consciously *decide* what to do rather than let circumstances completely dominate the agenda. One can consciously and deliberately become more dedicated to and skillful in the art of prayer. Paradoxically it is in prayer that one can become more intentional and deliberate as to how one will use his or her gifts, particularly those of one's own personality and time.

Liturgical prayer, the public expression of one's faith as a member of the community, offers a particularly rich opportunity for older persons. While lifelong patterns will influence the way in which a person participates, there is ample evidence that older persons can enter into the liturgy more fully and enthusiastically than the young. The experience of the Catholic community since Vatican Council II is instructive. While there are those who bemoan the loss of Latin and familiar structures, older persons seem to have adjusted to the changes particularly well. Many have adapted easily and enthusiastically to the changes that call for greater participation and creativity. There seems to be a similar experience in the Episcopal Church, as older members have accepted the ordination of women and the new Prayer Book at least as well as their younger counterparts.

The ministry *of* the older person as well as *to* the older person is receiving increasing attention. The next chapter of this book focuses on opportunities for such ministry.

A discussion of this nature would be incomplete without some mention of the ministry to those who are most frail and vulnerable. While the concept of chaplaincy service in the acute care setting has developed substantially in recent years, both through acceptance of pastoral care as a valid part of health care and through better preparation of those who do it, the ministry to the frail and disabled has not kept pace.

There are chaplaincy services in some long-term care programs, but they are the exception rather than the rule. Outreach from congregations to shut-ins could benefit from renewed commitment and fresh ideas. Too often, among clergy and laity alike, the pastoral role is perceived in such stereotypical terms that its healing energies are vitiated. Pastoral care of the frail elderly seems to be in its infancy, requiring our most thoughtful nurture.

We cannot exhaust the list of challenges generated by this new world of ours in these pages. They go across the board, open enormous possibilities, incur vast responsibilities. But each can be informed, illumined by a single guiding principle—reverence not only for life, but for the quality of life. We need only remember that we are called by our Lord to live more abundantly! This must define our Ethic for the Third Age.

Challenge to Ministry: Opportunities for Older Persons

Emma Lou Benignus

These thoughts concerning older adults, their roles and responsible participation in society, are addressed to the churches. Therefore, we turn to our Jewish-Christian heritage for an understanding of the possible, rather than only to secular data and theories of aging. Let the reader be warned: We shall explore the questions that arise with a bias we proudly own.

It is to be hoped that in the decade of the eighties the churches' concept of ministry of the laos (the whole people of God) will:

• Recognize that the most elderly, as well as the young, are potential channels of God's grace;

• Realize that spiritual gifts and the fruit of the Spirit are given by the Holy Spirit to old people, too, for their fulfillment and for their use in ministry;

• Be supportive of old people's yearnings to relate and to contribute;

• Be aware that a person can be born anew at any age.

When asked what they wish, rather than what they need, many older persons say, "To make a contribution," "To let the remaining years count," and even "To help my family by dying well." A woman of eighty-five who had just heard a prognosis of her imminent death turned from her doctor to her priest to say, "Being dead

24

and gone doesn't bother me, but what I do want is to make it clear to people that life lived here with God is every bit worth living all the way through. I don't want to contradict that in any way. If I begin to garble that message, will you help me keep it straight?

Note that this old woman:

- Realizes her way of living and dying can convey a message about God;
- Is quite clear about the statement she wants her life to make, that *with God* life is good;
- Knows she might, in spite of her intentions, betray the best she knows;
- Looks to her fellow Christian to help keep her faithful.

To have a mission, a purpose, a contribution to make and "promises to keep," and to want to come through to the last of one's days with integrity are the activity of the Spirit within. The physical limitations of aging may actually enhance this inner life. "Physical decline may limit productivity, but the activity of the Spirit continues through shifting the central focus of personal identity from doing-in-the-world to being-in-the-world, from what one does to who one is. As physical activity diminishes, the movement of the Spirit is toward an emphasis upon the nonphysical aspects of life. We all know individuals who in the face of seemingly overwhelming physical disintegration still face life with vitality that clearly is not based in their physical wellbeing. This vitality is evidence of their Spirit at work. It is plainly recognizable in the later years of life."[1]

To fail to engage this Spirit or carelessly to deny a person's capacity to serve is to consign that individual to loneliness and close down a life before its natural time.

The experience of an aged man comes to mind. Early one morning he was found peeling potatoes and humming to himself in the kitchen of the "home" in which he lived. Curtly reprimanded for his intrusion and punished by being confined to his room for the rest of the day, he muttered, "A man's got to be a man to live." Here it was: the yen to "be up and at it," the desire to do something of value, the longing to take part in life as others do. Do we nurture these values in childhood only to quell them in old age? We need to understand that, deprived of significant living, many die spiritually before their physical death.

We know a ninety-eight-year-old, tormented by an unpredictable heart and limited sight, who struggles daily to transcend her situation. She longs to walk outdoors, visiting the places in the garden and woods of the nursing home that have become dear to her, to feel the sunlight and wind on her body. But for safety's sake she has been forbidden to leave the porch unless someone walks with her. That someone seldom comes. On a particularly fresh day, as she leaned sadly against the porch screen, memory carried her back to a childhood visit to the zoo. She felt again the distress of seeing a chimpanzee confined to its cage when it so clearly wanted out, to do what monkeys do, to swing in the trees of the monkey yard as the others were. Now their lives were painfully alike, that chimp's and hers.

She returned to the living room, where a cheery soul said, "It's lovely out in the yard today, isn't it, Helen?" To her surprise she heard herself say, "Don't bother to call me Helen, just call me Chimp." With a laugh, and a tear on her cheek, she went to her room. What did she do there? With tears flowing copiously now, she beseeched God to care for the innocent animals of this world—all those destroyed by our pollution and greed in the arrogant conviction that they belong to us rather than to their Creator. Then she sent a check to a young grandnephew, asking him to plant a tree in some spot where children might play in its shade and birds build their nests in its branches.

This kind of loving interplay with all that is is one of the Spirit's gifts to older people. Out of their own pain and longing comes a heightened sensitivity to the needs of others. When society diminishes these persons' self-esteem by viewing them only as recipients with nothing to contribute, it takes away hope and meaning. We might ascribe such error to social ignorance of human nature. But when the church of Jesus Christ, who gave his life for others and calls us to do likewise, persistently supports only ministry *to* rather than also ministry *by* the elderly, it compounds society's sin.

The year 1935 marked the beginning of Social Security and the arbitrary designation of sixty-five as the age for mandatory retirement. It was expected that retirement with a modicum of assured income would give opportunity for the freedom to pursue one's choices. It was not expected that retirement would carry social opprobrium, or the message, "You're through now, someone else is replacing you. Forget all this and have a good time . . . somewhere else." Many negatives were suddenly linked with the sixty-fifth year. American society, including the churches, has on the whole accepted this negation of human resourcefulness with dehumanizing indifference.

But now the rapid increase in the number of people sixty-five and over who enjoy good health and are mentally alert is turning apathy into protest. "Retire at sixty-five to sit around for thirty years? Not I!" Initiatives that express the emancipation of the elderly are having an impact. Magazines feature articles on America's "lively generation," people in their "spectacular eighties" who "celebrate the silver."[2] There are among us now persons seventy, eighty, even ninety who are cultivating their talents, continuing their careers or launching into new ones, identifying capacities they never knew they had and going back to school for the joy of learning. The stereotypes and myths are being put to rout. People are beginning to recognize that sixty-five can launch a time of precious freedom to become reacquainted with ourselves, to follow the leading of the heart, the leading of the Spirit, and once again to play. Our younger years, with their heavy stress on success, status, making money, acquiring a home and family, tended to be shaped by external prescriptions and peer-conditioned values. We often found ourselves involved in decisions we would have preferred not to make, participating in programs and enterprises we could not personally endorse. But now, at retirement age, we approach a freedom heretofore unclaimed.

It is unfortunate, to say the least, when the local church does nothing at the time of a parishioner's retirement to remind that person that every member of the body of Christ by virtue of Holy Baptism is drawn into the company of the Spirit, the church, and that every member therein is endowed with charisms, gifts of grace, and significant spiritual capacities to be used for the good of all.[3] "To each is given the manifestation of the Spirit for the common good" (1 Cor. 12:7). If churches were to take seriously the apostle Paul's assurance of spiritual gifts, and if it became established practice for congregations to help their members identify, use, and enjoy these gifts, no Christian would need to fear that the years ahead will have to be uninvolved and meaningless.

The church's role is to awaken each of us to our giftedness. With Paul, it must say, "I remind you to rekindle the gift of God that is within you" (2 Tim. 1:6). To each man and woman of whatever age, the caring friends in the congregation might say, "Find out who you really are, for you are made in the *image of God.* Discern how God has been present in your life all these years. How does God call you now to be friend and servant, relating with Jesus Christ to the world God loves?" The privileged role of Christian friends in the congregation is to support the retiree, to recognize that "God did not give a spirit of timidity but a spirit of power and love and self-control." In such circumstances, with fellow Christians we can find the courage to take on our share of both joy and suffering for the sake of the Gospel of God who "called us with a holy calling, not in virtue of our works but in virtue of his own purpose and the grace which he gave us in Christ Jesus ages ago" (2 Tim. 1:7,9).

With such reminders stirring them to action, a group of older church women became active in the civil rights movement in the 1960s. They gathered momentum and supporters as they moved through the communities. Their dignity and informed declarations on behalf of civil rights and justice for all citizens gave others the courage to speak out, too. Several found themselves in jail, two of them wives of retired bishops and one the mother of a state governor. In a newspaper interview they expressed the wonder they found in being older and being free to witness to the values and conditions they hoped would prevail throughout the country, not only for the sake of the deprived but also for the sake of their own grandchildren and their children, that all might be free to become the persons God endows them to be.

These women gave classic expression through their civil rights ministry to the mark of maturity identified by psychologist Erik Erikson in his well-known account of human development, *Childhood and Society.* As people move through their years they come into different stages of concern and openness. These psychologically more mature tend to develop concern for the welfare of oncoming generations, as opposed to a primary fascination with their own good. Erikson's term for this capacity is "generativity," the gift of caring about the good of those yet to come. Another capacity that marks maturity as reported by Erikson is the desire for personal integrity, for life to be authentic, for coherence between professed values and life as actually lived. This yearning comes through in common parlance as a desire to set the record straight, to be accountable for one's life. When passions such as these dominate our later years, it is not surprising that the heart and conscience of many older people are opened afresh to the Christian gospel. Wellsprings of love and commitment deeper than ever before can be known in these years—and usually go untended.

As one reads the Hebrew and Christian Testaments, it is easy to gain the impression that when God wanted to bring about a significant change in the world, old people were called to the fore. Abraham and Sarah, both in their nineties, were the channels through whom God began a lineage of Israelites. When Israel was captive in Egypt, Moses and his brother Aaron, already in their sixties, were summoned to lead and console the people in their forty years of wandering in the desert. When something utterly new was about to break upon the world, the elderly Elizabeth and Zechariah were entrusted with the birth and rearing of John who became the Baptist, heralder of his cousin Jesus.

The older man Joseph was given to Mary as husband, ostensibly to protect her in a situation too daunting for youth. After the angel's annunciation to young Mary, she "went in haste" to spend three months with Elizabeth and Zechariah, one assumes in order to steady herself in faith through the company and wisdom of this older couple. When the infant Jesus was presented in the temple, it was old Simeon, staving off death, who first recognized him as the awaited Messiah and who warned Mary that her heart would be pierced by her son's suffering (Luke 2:34-35). And then the very old prophetess Anna, long cloistered in the Temple, when she saw Jesus "gave thanks to God" and went out to speak of him to all who were looking for the redemption of Jerusalem. Not only were these older persons vehicles of divine action, but they spoke prophetically through canticles and hymns that have become part of the treasured liturgy of the Western church: Zechariah's Benedictus (Luke 1:78-79), Simeon's Nunc Dimittis (Luke 2:29-32).

31

John Koenig, professor at Union Theological Seminary, wrote in his sensitive essay *The Older Person's Worth in the Eyes of God* that in Luke's gospel

New things happen to older people. . . . [They] receive a vital ministry to perform for Israel, precisely in their last days. In fact, it is only in old age that they come to experience their true vocation. . . .

In Luke's treatment of older people we do not find the conventional expectation encountered in most cultures . . . that the aged are primarily bearers and guardians of ancient wisdom. No, according to Luke, God chooses old people as bearers and proclaimers of the New Creation. They are visionaries, futurists, people charismatically gifted with a clearer picture of God's unfolding plan than their younger brothers and sisters.

Koenig finds in Paul's New Testament letters similar presentation of elderly persons as trailblazers and adventurers in God's creation. Paul himself was sixty when he planned his new and most extensive ministry in Spain (Romans 15:22-29). Summing up his findings about old and young in scripture, John Koenig gives these comments:

The young see visions, they are intoxicated by novelty. Age helps them to distinguish between true and false novelty . . . a pseudo-radicalism which actually wants to cut itself off from all roots. For Luke, older persons exercise a prophetic ministry which enables young people to see the "big picture" of God's plan for salvation. . . .

In spite of losses and physical disability degeneration is not the core of reality. For Christians, the really real is transformation, a daily re-sensitizing of ourselves to the . . . goodness of God out of which new ministries by older persons can emerge. No one is too old to experience a blossoming of charismatic gifts for ministry. No one's life is too far gone to become a place for the Spirit's empowering self-disclosure.[4]

In his seventies Senator Hubert Humphrey bore testimony to the Spirit's power for ennobling self-disclosure by an older person and the value this has for the young. When he was free of responsibility to the administration of which he long had been a part, the senator acknowledged that his deepest intuitive insights had warned him of the folly of the Vietnam war and that he profoundly regretted not heeding the word he had heard spoken deep inside himself. The courage of this public confession by a revered senior statesman has itself been a continuing word of inspiration, integrity, and hope for old and young alike at this time of intense value confusion.

Senator Humphrey's story brings to mind the encounter between the incredulous elder Nicodemus and Jesus in John's Gospel (John 3:1-6). Jesus said that to "see" the kingdom of God one must be born anew (reoriented). To this Nicodemus, obviously thinking of physical birth, asked "How can a man be born when he is old?" Can a senior citizen be born anew? Indeed! The issue for Jesus here is nothing less than transformation, change in a person's inner life so radical as to be described as a new birth, possible at any age for those who are open to the spirit of the ever-creating God. "The wind blows where it wills," among old and young, rich and poor, strong and weak. Barclay's commentary on John's Gospel describes the effect: "It is to have something happen to the soul which can only be described as being born all over again; and the whole process is not a human achievement because it comes from the grace and power of God."

Through God's great mercy it is possible in the midst of the threatening insecurities of old age to let go, to let the perishable, the transitory, however dear to us, be "washed clean away" by grace. It is possible to turn from all the illusory "saviors" one has clung to throughout life and abandon one's self in faith. The highly vulnerable later decades, with their incomparable, unpredictable, often uncontrollable experiences are usually life's most fertile field for sensitivity to the Spirit, and for sinking our roots ever more deeply into the fullest possible personal relationship with Jesus Christ. In loving him we do not stop cherishing people and situations and things dear to the heart. On the contrary, the heart expands to cherish all of creation as our Lord does. Carl Jung called the lifelong years of aging life's spiritual journey. At midlife, according to Jung, we shift from an initial acquisitive posture to one of relinquishment, voluntary or involuntary. The element of trust at this point is imperative. In trust, we can be free to reply, "Yes, Lord, let your will, not mine, be done. I will follow to the end of my days." Then, regardless of age, the Spirit will provide the capacities required, and may even indulge the faithful with gifts of amazing grace.

Opportunities for ministry change with the changing times and circumstances of the older person. The old cliche about "where there's a will, there's a way" is often proved valid. What God makes of our offering, however small, is God's business, as is illustrated in Mark 12:43-44. A poor widow gave two small coins, and Jesus said to his disciples, "This poor widow has put in more than all those who are contributing to the treasury. For they all contributed out of their abundance; but she out of her poverty has put in everything she had." As we give to others all that we have left to give—a hand wave, a smile, a look of gratitude, a word of praise—and offer it in Jesus' name, we take part in ministry. A woman on the edge of blindness, with very little left of a once abundant life, begins her day by standing at her window where all she sees is a bit of light and praises God for the gift of life. "It is wonderful so to enjoy God's riches," she says. Her daily prayers of praise and the love she radiates pervade the home where she resides.

The book *I Can Still Pray*[5] speaks of the spiritual capacities of the elderly. It is a tribute to a woman whose body had been deteriorating for twenty-one years. Now, after yet another stroke, she was physically helpless. When a visitor began to commiserate, she countered optimistically, "But I can still pray." In circumstances of extreme limitation she found purpose for her life and reminded her visitor that she retained the most basic of functions for a God-related, faith-filled life—the capacity to pray!

Because he believed in the reality of spiritual power, a young minister wanted as much of it as possible circulating in the congregation. So he invited the six housebound members of the church to form a prayer team with him. Every Sunday the morning service is taped and delivered, along with copies of the intercession list, to each team member. Although separated, the team has a corporate prayer time every morning when the priest is saying the daily office. Throughout the rest of the day they offer prayers for people on the intercession list or hold them before God in meditation. The priest and team meet weekly by means of a telephone conference, and he spends an hour with each of them every six weeks to discuss their own spiritual development. Currently, one of the men on the team is helping a recent convert learn to pray. One of the women has a small prayer and Bible study group that meets regularly in her home.

How superb it is when the seasoned members of the congregation take new clergy and their spouses under a welcoming wing, to retell the story of the parish's history, distinguish between its sacred traditions and its sacred cows, alert them to areas of sensitivity, and befriend them with the trust, hope, and candor that can grow in the aging years. Most important of all, there could be prayers daily for the new leaders, that they be faithful and a conduit of blessing for all.

Five years ago the Episcopal church introduced *Age in Action* in the church schools. Each teacher was urged to invite an older person or two to share a class session, giving young and old a chance to interact. In some churches this has become an avenue of continuing intergenerational contact in a setting where the norm separates the ages for learning. In class, children and elderly can pray together and discuss that about which they pray. In imagination they can relive Bible stories, envisioning themselves as companions of Jesus, and then talk about the experience. With activities of this sort, the Scriptures and the faith journey become meeting ground for the generations. Those who for years have served the altar and cared for its adornments can teach the young.

For older adults who come to church, an occasional opportunity for a leadership role is important not only for them but for the rest of the congregation as well. A lay reader who could no longer climb steps read the lesson from his pew with the aid of a microphone. A long-retired rector, still dear to the congregation, was invited back for homecoming Sunday. Now in a wheelchair, he preached from the center aisle. His very presence was a gift to young and old alike. Practical solutions to difficult situations can always be found, if the desire is there.

A widow, desperate with pain over her husband's sudden death when they were both seventy, continued to "pray a psalm a day" as they had done all their married life. But now she also read the psalm aloud to transcribe it on tape. When the tape was filled she gave it and a small recorder to a widowed blind man all but lost in grief not unlike hers. Her reaching out to him was the beginning of his return to sociability and later to the church.

The losses of later life cannot be escaped, but they can be transcended to become occasions of spiritual growth as we learn to incorporate them into ministry on behalf of others. In a profound sort of way, ministry is not really an option; it is an essential expression of the nature of our being, an avenue of our fulfillment, our response to being made in the image and likeness of God.

In God's amazing way with us, when needs arise the answer is usually already there somewhere, "waiting in the bush" as was the ram when God asked Abraham to give up Isaac. There is great need today for the loving care of young children, as mounting economic pressures send more mothers to work and as single-parent families proliferate. The incidence of child abuse increases steadily. Where is the answer? In part it may lie in matching these patterns with another social phenomenon—the largest number of available grandparents and great-grandparents in good health our society has ever seen. We need each other.

In Eastern and Southern cultures, as well as in traditional Black society, the grandparenting role is assumed as a dependable component of the family's life. Our housing patterns and industrial mobility, plus our affluence, have separated the generations in this country. Thus there is a great opportunity for many older men and women to lend a hand to working parents and their children as surrogate grandparents. A new form of three-generational ministry, called Family Friends, has been launched by the National Council on the Aging in Washington, D.C. Volunteers are in homes one to three times a week to be with young children, or the chronically ill, or disabled, to relieve the family caregivers. Participants in this program can be reimbursed for expenses, travel, and meals, so that none who are willing need to be deprived of the opportunity to give of themselves.[6]

There is more value and carryover influence than meets the eye in this kind of relationship. From a survey of professional colleagues, the author of this article discovered that, when seeking inspiration and value, the memory turns to a grandparent or grandparent surrogate more frequently than to any other significant person. Psychological studies show that bonding between the first and third generation tends to be smoother, more endorsing, and more enduring. The suggestion has been made that if generations seek to live together, the first and third might do better than the first and second. The ministry of hospitality was lauded in Jesus' day. Can the senior members of our society restore it? Last summer the Church of the Brethren made travel for families easier by staking out a trail across the country of Brethren households available for bed and breakfast. Many of the host homes were those of older adults with rooms to spare and time to be hospitable. A program for family members visiting hospitalized patients was started by the hospital's Pink Ladies team (mostly older adults) who knew peers nearby with houses now shorn of family of their own. Owners who were willing to become hosts and hostesses were given guidance for opening their home to paying guests. They also received training in responding to persons in bereavement.

The need for voluntary service in our society is as wide as the imagination can conceive. The Shepherd Center in Kansas City, Missouri, is a Methodist program that matches the skills of senior volunteers with needs in the community. In England, where cash flow is generally much less than here, the parishes have instituted Barter Societies. An older man will dig the garden in exchange for some of the landlady's canned produce after the crop is harvested. A crippled woman will care for two small children in exchange for their mother doing her shopping and laundry. Once a month everyone involved in the Barter Society goes to church and stays for a small meal with the rest of the folks.

In the United States our approximation of the Barter Society is the Self-Help Group Movement. About 3,000 self-help groups now exist, with members helping one another by providing friendly support, understanding, skills, practical information, and the kind of consolation and encouragement that can be given by someone who "has been there." These groups recognize that everybody needs support systems and that systems we had long counted on are now eroding due to changes in society, new family patterns, legislation, and various factors beyond our control. These "talk-it-over" and "lend-a-hand" groups are voluntary. They meet in churches, community centers, homes, sometimes with a professional invited to provide special training. But for the most part, members help one another, as friends do, by drawing on their own accumulated resourcefulness.[7]

The role of teacher's helper in some public schools attracts older volunteers. Their stories are sometimes poignant. A lonely, widowed retiree responded to the school's SOS for helpers. He was assigned to a class whose teacher suggested, "Come and just be around, take it as it happens." One day a withdrawn eight-year-old girl attached herself to him, saying nothing but staying close. Eventually, in bits and pieces, she told her story of sexual abuse, physical neglect, and isolation in her own home. Thanks to this quietly listening grandfather, the child was rescued. Another child, a hyperactive boy who when left alone could not concentrate enough to learn, found a friend in an older volunteer who sat with him and calmly, patiently talked with him. In this aura of quiet, loving, daily attention the boy could do his work and learn.

Older volunteers have the gifts of time and love to share. From them the emotionally disturbed, affection-starved, acting-out children who can turn a classroom into turmoil may receive the attentive care they need—care that cannot be bought.

Concern for the quality of education is prominent in the conversation of a church retirement community on the West Coast. An eighty-four-year-old said, "Let's not just talk about it, let's do something about it!" There now exists a "writing alliance" between a group of retirees interested in writing and an equal number of young people from a nearby school. They meet regularly to share their work and critique it. Comradery, mutual respect, and self-esteem are nurtured in this intergenerational venture. In addition, the art of writing, grossly neglected today, gets good support. We underscore this experience as an excellent illustration of how a value recognized as important by the senior generation can be activated in the young when the two generations experience it together.

Many older adults find gratification and meaning in reaching out to others in a wondrous variety of services and supportive enterprises. Others, in numbers gradually increasing, are involving themselves in issues and situations where political, social, institutional, or legal change is necessary to assure justice and peace at home and abroad and to further the public good. Older people with discretionary time are sitting in on city council and school board meetings, and in sessions of environmental protection agencies and public-health boards, to check chicanery or to further much needed two-way communication between such agencies and the general public. Still others organize for public attention and change.

Two retired men, one concerned about what is happening to our trees and the other a skilled fisherman concerned about polluted water causing cancerous fish, spoke of their interests with several Boy Scout troops from whose membership a nucleus of Young Citizens Concerned has been formed. This is "generativity" at work in the best of ways, young and old together caring about God's world.

Many religious groups and individuals concerned about public affairs, ecology, health, and other issues find that the adult courses developed by the American Association of Retired Persons are excellent resources available at no cost, ready for leaders in churches, local libraries, and clubs to use. A retired high school principal responded to one of these, the 55-Alive driver training program designed to help senior citizens be safe drivers. He corralled twenty-five retired colleagues from church and school contacts to set up the course in four Illinois counties. Now it has spread throughout the state and met with such success that the Illinois state legislature presently assured a 10 percent reduction in insurance premiums to those who pass the course. The 55-Alive program was conceived by older people, for older people, and is taught by them. The Illinois law was passed as a result of lobbying by older citizens. Older adults in action to save lives!

Twenty-six denominations maintain a Washington, D.C., office for government relations, with some of their work done by volunteer legislative assistants. Older adults apply for these positions, which provide excellent training in legislature and political processes, valuable preparation for a leadership role back home where voting counts. The elderly have a larger percentage of voters than any other age group. In addition to the voting box, there is always the mailbox, an implement increasingly used for today's participation in sociopolitical change. Human justice and world survival issues merit much more attention than they usually receive in the churches. Where are the elderly as active agents in creating a better future? Is this their role? We affirm it is uniquely their role. Their disestablishment is a gift, an opportunity to dream of a new order, to pursue visions of new structures and ways of functioning as well as new alliances to replace the tightening knots of injustice and self-concern, discrimination, and greed.

As they emerge from cocoons of dependency and self-doubt, the aging begin to become themselves—persons with strong instincts for the good of coming generations, with compassion for humanity deepened by their own losses and suffering through the years. They are clear about the futility of relying on material and physical realities for dependable security or salvation, and they are old enough to have experienced through repeated wars the madness of the military approach to world peace. We have among us many models of the integrity, the courage, and the faithful selflessness of Spirit-led older persons. They come from all cultures and every economic level. Let us form the most heterogeneous groupings we can, to learn to hear each other, to discover the contributions each can make to further the freedom and well-being of all people. Who and what can stop older adults? Nothing except their own lethargy. God has given to generous numbers the privilege of surviving —a gift to be used for the larger creation, not just in self-interest.

By the year 2020 there will be forty million people over sixty in the United States and nearly six hundred million in the world. If we exist at all by then, mobilization for a new world order will be under way *by negotiation.* We believe "that the new world order can be promoted by older people, the group most free to do it."[8] If the ministry of older people can become *prophetic* as well as existential, older members then can serve the world as the Spirit's instruments of social transformation. We return to Nicodemus: Can an old person be reborn?

As God wrestled with Jacob and David, so the Spirit seeks to wrestle with us to the very end, winning us from ego-centeredness to Christ Jesus' way of life. Although the University of Michigan is a secular institution, it believes that older citizens can learn new ways to be builders of community and laborers for peace. So it offers institutes for training in communication skills and personal growth that are open to people all ages. Can the church be content to do less?

As surely as God gives gifts to the elderly, the elderly are intended to give gifts of themselves to the world.

It is the role of the churches to nurture the ministries of their members, whatever their age.

Notes

1. "Spirituality During Aging" by Ernest G. Hall, Epping, N.H. (unpublished paper presented at the 36th Annual Scientific Meeting of the Gerontological Society of America, San Francisco, 1983).
2. "The Spectacular Sixties," *Modern Maturity,* Dec. 1983, pp. 55-58.

3. *Discover Your Gifts,* Workbook, Christian Reformed House Missions, Grand Rapids, Mich. 49560, 1983.
4. *The Older Persons' Worth: A Theological Perspective,* Presbyterian Senior Services, N.Y., N.Y., 1980. (Symposium at Union Theological Seminary)
5. *I Can Still Pray,* C. W. Peckham and A. B. Peckham, Otterbein Home, Lebanon, Ohio, 1979. (Out of print.)
6. Write Family Friends, Project Director, 600 Maryland Ave. S.W., Washington, D.C. 20024.
7. Write New Jersey Self-Help Clearinghouse Nationwide, Saint Clare's Hospital, Denville, N.J. 07834.
8. "Aging and World Order," Jim Baines, *The Whole Earth Papers,* No. 13, Global Education Association, 552 Park Avenue, East Orange, N.J. 07017.

Meditation and Prayer
Nancy Roth

As we approach our later years, reflect on the events of our past, and ponder the years to come, we may feel an increasing need for something that gives meaning to our lives. The exploration of meditation and prayer offers not only the possibility of finding meaning but a path of unexpected adventure.

That adventure begins with a deepening sense of our identity as human beings. In Genesis 2:7 we read the wonderful word picture in which God scoops up a handful of dust and then breathes life into it: ". . . . then the Lord God formed man of dust from the ground, and breathed into his nostrils the breath of life; and man became a living being."

First, we *are* dust. Our bodies are not to be ignored! Whether we have colic as newborns, chicken pox as eight-year-olds, acne as adolescents, hypertension as adults, or cataracts as elders, we are continuously reminded that we are dust. The physical sensations of a full stomach, of restorative sleep, of quickened energy, and of calmness of body all touch our spirits as well. Religious teachings that urge us to despise or ignore our bodies just do not work for us, either in a practical sense or in the framework of a Christianity that proclaims the Incarnation—God become flesh—as a central doctrine.

But we are more than our bodies. There is in us a capacity for that which is not of us. In Genesis, we are told that it is God's life itself. We can grow more and more open to "that within us that is not of us" as we step back a bit from the bustle of our middle years. The increased leisure of our later years is apt to make us confront our emptiness. That confrontation can lead either to despair and loneliness or to God, as we identify God's breath as that for which the space or emptiness within us yearns.

The story of Genesis 2 tells us that the basic reality about us is the reality of our relationship to God. Our identity, it tells us, rests not in our function in the workplace or in society, but in who we are in relation to God. It is an identity that we discover ever more deeply in prayer, an identity that cannot ever be taken away from us, either in life or in death.

Who am I? *I am dust, animated by the Spirit of God.* We share that identity with every other human being in the world; they are our brothers and sisters. We must accept their individuality and uniqueness, as we must accept our own. Our dust is, if you will, the raw material of our personalities and our physiques, our gifts and our shortcomings. It is *our* dust, not anyone else's, that we are meant to bring before God. To accept that fact can unleash a tremendous zest for living.

Questions for Reflection

• What are some of the roles I have had in life? How has it felt when I have had to shed them?

- When in my life have I sensed my identity as "dust"? How does my body feel when I am anxious? Afraid? Under tension? Relaxed? Happy? Excited?
- When have I sensed "that within me that is not of me"? Have I been moved by beauty, or the love of other people? Have crisis, loss, or anxiety brought me face to face with an inner emptiness? Have I ever been aware of a yearning for God?
- When have I been most deeply aware of my unity with other human beings? What is unique about me? What are my gifts and shortcomings? How would I describe my temperament and my life situation? Do I accept this raw material or try to ignore or reject it?

Breath is a rhythm, and the life of prayer is a rhythm also, a two-fold pattern of giving and receiving, exhaling and inhaling. We prepare ourselves (exhale) so that God can fill us (inhale). Most of us have discovered this rhythm in the pattern of deaths and rebirths or valleys and mountains that we experience as we travel through life. However, while the rhythm is a natural one, it is something of which we need to be continuously reminded. Times of prayer and meditation are a deliberate return to that space at the center of our beings where we are reminded of our relationship with God.

The Christian tradition teaches that prayer ranges from verbal prayer (prayer with words) through meditation (reflective prayer) to contemplation (wordless prayer). Most people feel an affinity for one or another of these kinds of prayer, but we need to know them all. There will be particular times in our lives when we need to call upon one particular way. Sometimes, for instance, we need the structure of words. Sometimes we feel utterly unable to use them.

Although St. Paul and others urge us to "pray without ceasing," this does not come easily.

If regular prayer is not already a part of your life, I suggest setting a specific time, anywhere from ten minutes to an hour or more. Deliberately create a *space* in every sense of the word; *privacy*, a space where you will not be interrupted; *time*, a space when you will not think of other duties; *inner relaxation*, an attitude of psychological space.

Physical Readiness for Prayer

It is helpful to begin your prayer time with focusing on the body and how it feels. The *dust* must settle! Some people find that swimming or walking is helpful, for example. The point is to recognize and to learn to release the physical tension which often blocks our permitting God's life to breathe in us. The following exercises may be helpful. Use any that suit your body, bearing in mind that the approach is that of body-awareness and relaxation, not calisthenics. (If you have any physical problems modify these exercises according to your doctor's advice.)

Either standing or sitting in a straight chair with your legs apart, stretch toward the ceiling, first with one arm, then the other. Repeat slowly and gently four times, then stretch with both arms and inhale. Exhale and let the arms drop; then let the head drop. Let the weight of the head bring the spine forward. If you are seated in a chair, let the head fall between your knees. If you are standing, let the spine fall forward as far as is comfortable. Stay in that position a moment, then slowly build up the spine again, vertebra by vertebra. When you are straight, imagine that someone has a string attached to the top of your head (toward the back, in line with the spine) and is pulling it towards the ceiling. Grow!

Circle the head to the right, so that the right ear is toward the right shoulder, then to the back, towards the left, then forwards. Repeat. Reverse the circle. Repeat. Again stretch the head, neck, and spine towards the ceiling by means of the imaginary string. Then bring the shoulders forward, raise them towards the ears, pull them back, and let them drop. Repeat. Then pull the shoulders back, raise them towards the ears, bring them forward, and let them drop. Repeat.

Choose a position comfortable for prayer, in which you feel relaxed yet alert. Some people like to sit on a chair, feet flat on the floor or crossed at the ankles, palms up on the lap. Be aware of the weight of your body.

Now picture the tension draining from each part of the body in turn, beginning with your feet. (The right foot, the right calf, the right thigh, the left foot, etc.) Next become aware of your breath. Breathe through the nostrils, trying to breathe as you did when a baby, relaxing the abdomen on the inhalation and drawing it in on the exhalation.

Your body should now feel tranquil and relaxed.

The traditional first category of prayer is *verbal prayer* or prayer with words (sometimes called *vocal prayer*). These words can be your own and spontaneous or the words of others. The English teacher of prayer Evelyn Underhill kept a notebook of prayers she especially loved. You may wish to make a practice of saying special prayers found in books of worship of various denominations and monastic orders. Such use of the words of others helps us remember that our prayers, even when said in private, are part of a great community stretching across the world and across the centuries.

Honest conversation with God covers the whole spectrum of our life. We are talking with a God who loves us enough to have become one of us. There is *nothing* we need hold back from such a God.

Verbal or conversational *prayer* may be used throughout the day. Repairing furniture or folding laundry for your family, you may silently hold each person before God. Fishing or knitting or washing the dishes, you may let your mind review and pray about the day's events. As prayer becomes more and more habitual, you will find that what might be humdrum tasks or mindless activities can often be transformed into opportunities for prayer.

While we can relate to God through words alone, we soon find that words also provide a starting point for reflection.

An Exercise in Verbal and Reflective Prayer

Adoration: Think of God's life moving through you with each breath. Enjoy God's nearness to you and God's being beyond anything you can imagine.

Praise: When in your life have you had a sense of God's presence and care, God's being with and within you? How did you feel then? Like singing and dancing? Like expressing your love for God in some other way?

Thanksgiving: What specific things in your life move you to thanksgiving? Spouse, children, grandchildren, friends, or the memories associated with them? The beauty of the earth? A measure of good health? The knowledge of God's love for you as revealed in the gift of Jesus Christ?

Oblation (Self-giving): Offer yourself for the working out of God's purposes. Reflect on whether you *accept* yourself. God doesn't want a half-hearted gift. God wants you as you are, as well as how you are called to be.

Intercession (Prayer for others): There are so many needs in the world that you may feel overwhelmed. Try to discern what needs particularly move you. They may be international in scope (some people pray with the front page of the newspaper before them) or a personal list of people you feel called to hold before God. As you become increasingly sensitive to the life of the Spirit working within your own life, you will find this kind of prayer becoming more and more spontaneous: a movement of the soul as you pass the bag lady on the sidewalk, read a disturbing headline, or find concern for a friend welling up inside.

Intercession thrusts us into the context of the *communion of saints,* a way of talking about our unity with other people, in life and in death. Many people have had the experience of becoming quiet in preparation for prayer and finding the thought of another person coming to the surface of their consciousness, along with a powerful inner demand to pray for that person. Such an occurence gives us a hint about what we mean when we say that God prays in us. We begin to realize that somehow, in a way beyond human understanding, intercession—indeed, all prayer—is our cooperation with the rhythm of God's life in relation to the world.

Petition (Prayer for your own needs): What do you *really* need? Place your life, your needs, your fears, and your complaints before God. You need hold nothing back, for God knows all these things anyway.

Penitence: God calls us to our truest selves, but often we are deaf to that call or do not have the courage to answer it. What impedes God's breath moving through you? Wrong priorities? Deliberate sin? Thoughtlessness? What dark corners in your life have you not yet opened to healing? This part of your prayer is a time not for despair but a time to open yourself, as you are, to God's healing forgiveness, which is waiting for you. It is also a time to ask God to help us forgive others.

Trust: End your prayer with a quiet placing of all your thoughts, feelings, and hopes before God. You might think of this time of trustfulness as a deep relaxed breath or sigh of relief.

Meditation: In the traditional Christian sense, this means using our imagination and reason in seeking through prayer the meaning of a passage of Scripture for our own lives. One ancient method is called *lectio divina*: a rhythm of reading the Bible slowly, stopping to reflect, and moving more deeply into prayer, until one feels the urge to continue the reading, then once again move into reflecting and praying.

Prayer Exercise: Lectio Divina

Choose a place to begin (perhaps the beginning of one of the Gospels) and set aside at least twenty minutes. Read slowly. If a passage or word commands your attention, stop reading. Dwell on the word or passage. Let it become an opening or window through which the breath of God can come into your soul. Spend as long as you wish before that window. When you feel ready, read on, pausing again when you feel moved to do so.

During the sixteenth century, another way of meditating on Scripture was developed. It involved a more complex process of reflection upon a text. The best-known form of this type of meditation, developed by St. Ignatius of Loyola, is called the Ignatian method. The words originally used to describe the structure of this type of prayer were recollection, reading, using the imagination, memory, intellect and will, and resolution. A simpler process is indicated by four words: *prepare, picture, ponder,* and *permit.*

Prayer Exercise: Modified Ignatian Meditation

Prepare. The night before you plan this meditation, choose a passage of Scripture on which to meditate—preferably a story from the Old or New Testaments that contains a scene you can picture. Read it over slowly before you go to bed.

At the time you have set aside for the meditation (I would suggest twenty minutes to half an hour) relax physically, using some of the suggested exercises if they are helpful, and silently offer this time to God.

Read the passage over slowly.

Picture. Use the senses of sight, hearing, smell, taste, and touch. Be there in your imagination. Try to experience what happened through the experience of the original participants.

Ponder. Having entered the passage, let the passage enter you. What parallels do you see in your own life? Do you identify with a particular person or emotion in the passage? Is there a phrase that strikes you? Listen to the breath of God through the word of Scripture.

Permit. This is the point of the meditation where the response to prayer is made in terms of daily life. As a result of the meditation, is there a way you feel that you are called to permit God to work through you? Since this may well be a large and demanding insight, choose a small and symbolic action as an immediate response. It may be as simple as writing a letter, making a phone call, or finishing a long-neglected task. Or it may be that you will try to be conscious of God's energy breathing in you as you go about your tasks for just a single hour, or to be especially aware of one member of your household. Or you may wish to take away from your meditation a phrase to hold in your mind throughout the day. Conclude this part of the meditation with a quiet time in which you give thanks for this time of being in God's presence.

This Ignatian method of meditation may also be based on content other than Scripture. For instance, you may meditate on a natural object:

Prepare: Choose a shell, stone, pine cone or anything that captures your fancy. *Ponder:* Holding the object, use all your senses to explore it. Imagine that you are a child discovering it for the first time. What specifically strikes you? What memories does it evoke? What is it saying to you, in terms of your life? *Permit:* How might this meditation be expressed in your life, in an action or a change of attitude?

As you gain experience in meditation, you will find you can meditate upon a wide range of subjects, not only Scripture and natural objects, but works of art, incidents from your life, devotional writings, poetry, icons, and your dreams. It is a rich way of prayer that helps us integrate our thought processes, including our imagination and our life experience, in the act of moving into relationship with God. As with verbal prayer, meditation transforms us, as we learn to become more and more sensitive to God's messages in our lives, whether it is through the words we read or hear or through people and events. In this kind of prayer, we can move closer to the truth that there is nothing through which God cannot speak to us, if we but keep the channels open. Intentional meditation time is a time to learn how to open those channels.

During some of your prayer times, you may have experienced a moment of just resting in God's presence, without any particular reflective process going on. This is the mode of prayer the Christian tradition calls *contemplative prayer.* My favorite description of this prayer occurs in a story about a French priest, who, curious about a peasant whom he has seen praying in his little parish church for hours at a time, finally asks him what he does while he is praying. "Why, it's very simple," the peasant replies. "I just look at God, and God looks at me."

In spite of the apparent simplicity of contemplation as just described, Christian tradition has tended to consider it a form most suitable for those very advanced in prayer. But *everyone* is potentially a contemplative, for becoming attentive and responsive to the presence of God is what we were created for—why we are "restless" for God, in St. Augustine's words. The yearning for the experience of contemplation may be what accounts for the immense contemporary popularity of Eastern spiritualities and their secular offshoots. These spiritualities usually teach useful techniques of meditation or contemplative prayer, and the Christian church has been enriched by exposure to them.

The adventure of contemplation requires a measure of silence and solitude we may not have experienced before. Thoughts will inevitably flit across our minds, like birds on the horizon, and our attention must be gently brought back. It is important to realize that you are not likely to have the sense of accomplishment in this type of prayer that you may have felt in verbal prayer or meditation. It is rather like the desert, in contrast to the bustling city. You may at times have a powerful sense of the presence of God; at other times, you may experience emptiness and darkness, or simply faithful waiting. Contemplation demands trust in the goodness of the One whom we are seeking, and the courage and willingness to open ourselves to the love and acceptance we will find when we encounter that God. This is therefore not only the simplest but also the most difficult of the ways to pray, because it means giving up our own control. It is also potentially the most transforming of prayers. We might call contemplative prayer a "school of love" for as we rest in the presence of a loving God, we ourselves grow in the ability to love not only God, but ourselves and other people.

In exploring this way of praying, I suggest that you spend five to ten minutes quieting the body and the mind, then another twenty minutes in silence, focusing on whatever you have chosen, using some of the ideas below, knowing that the true focus beyond that is on the presence of God. The mind should not feel tense but relaxed; thoughts may come and go, but don't feel anxious about them. Simply offer this space in time and in your soul, and "just look at God" as "God looks at you."

Prayer Exercise: Contemplation

Preparation is particularly important in this type of prayer. Stretch, relax, and find a position in which your body is comfortable—but not so comfortable you will go to sleep! Begin always with awareness of your body and awareness of your breath, keeping in mind the image of God's breath breathing through you. Let your mind relax, and quietly offer this time to God.

You may wish to experiment over the course of some weeks with various ways of focusing the mind. Some persons are oriented toward movement, some toward words, some toward images, others toward what they touch or hear or smell. In reading my suggestions, bear in mind that learning about prayer reveals the incredible variety of human psychological makeup. Choose what is helpful and seems to lead you to God; gently leave behind what does not feel appropriate for you.

Focus on the breath: This is the simplest and therefore in a sense the most difficult. It will appeal to the kinetically-oriented, those who experience life most easily through movement. Center your attention on your breathing; think of God's breath as moving through you, and think of yourself as breathing in God's life and love and giving it back to God.

Focus on a mantra: A mantra is a word or phrase used as a focus in contemplative prayer. In using a mantra, coordinate the word or phrase with your breath, if you wish. Your mantra may express something about your relationship to God. It may be simply the word "God." It may be "Come Holy Spirit" on the inhalation and "I give myself to you" on the exhalation. A classic mantra is the *Jesus Prayer* of the Eastern Orthodox tradition: "Lord Jesus Christ, have mercy on me." You may prefer a phrase such as "Be still and know that I am God." Scripture, particularly the Psalms, contains many potential mantras; choose a phrase that combines meaning with rhythm.

Focus on an image: Some people find they quiet their minds best by focusing on either an inner or an outer image. Picture in your imagination a scene, indoors or outdoors, where you have experienced a sense of God's presence. Or picture our Lord, a symbolic shape, or a light. You may also actually look at a religious painting, a crucifix, a candle, or something that draws your attention and takes it God-wards. The tradition of icons in the Eastern church grew out of the practice of using such paintings as windows through which one gazed at the divine. A natural object may be used in contemplation, if you use it as a focus for attention, as you rest in the presence of the Creator.

Other points of focus: Touch—Holding a natural object, a rosary, or a crucifix. *Listening*—Chanting yourself, or listening to music that moves you to prayer or to the sounds around you. *Smell*—Incense, flowers, or a pine grove. *Taste*—Fresh-baked bread, eaten slowly. All of these methods demonstrate the reality of our dust: that our senses are a gateway to prayer, as we grow as whole people in our relationship to God.

The life of prayer includes both deliberate times of prayer and times when your life's activities themselves become prayerful. We all need to look realistically at the rhythm of our days to see if we have, indeed, set aside enough special time for prayer. Like the five-finger exercises that prepare for the piano sonata, or the barre exercises that warm up the dancer's muscles for the ballet, intentional prayer time establishes the rhythm of relationship with God that makes it possible to be our own most real selves in our daily life.

I suggest that instead of approaching the practice of prayer as a part of the day we think of it in another way: as the *center* of the day. Prayer is a return to your center. Therefore, it is the most important thing for you to do each day, despite the messages to the contrary of the society in which we live. Prayer helps us to live with a consciousness of God's presence that provides tranquility and purpose throughout our various activities. The

Christian spiritual tradition calls this habitual recollection—literally a *re*-collection of ourselves. It is the opposite of being scattered.

Finally, we need in this adventure to travel not alone, but with the support of another person or persons. Because our culture militates in both subtle and obvious ways against the values discussed in this chapter, we need to walk together as we seek our true identities as the men and women we are, beyond any of our roles, in relation to God.

If you are part of a worshiping community (a church or prayer group), you may already know the support and feeling of belonging that mutual prayer can give. Real prayer nurtures love in us and draws us towards others. It is helpful to have a *soul friend,* someone else committed to prayer, with whom you can compare notes, in person or by letter. You may wish to keep a journal or diary of your experiences as you undertake this adventure in prayer and to share some of them with your friend. You may decide to spend some time each week together in silence. You may wish to seek an experienced spiritual director for guidance. The tradition of spiritual direction is an ancient one in which interest has recently revived. A skilled spiritual director combines knowledge of the spiritual tradition with openness to the Spirit and thus helps others to grow in relationship with God.

Theophane, a Russian bishop of the nineteenth century, describes prayer as "standing before God with the mind in the heart." We have seen prayer as a process of moving from words to reflection to loving: from the mind to the heart. The last part of the process is surely our moving through all the phases of life, and beyond the gateway of death. Whatever we pray and however we pray, if prayer is an encounter with the Reality which is God, prayer will transform us. As we consciously return to our Center, again and again, we encounter the One who breathes life into us and gives us our deepest identities, which can never, by the events of life or by death, be taken from us. As we grow in relationship with that One in all the ways we pray, we become more and more certain that our adventure will be a never-ending one, in which we explore the joyous landscape that is the eternal life of God within our souls.

The Gift of Wisdom
Robert W. Carlson

Aging and Wisdom

In the third act of Verdi's opera *Ernani,* the Spanish
king Don Carlos is hiding in the tomb of his ancestor
Charlemagne. His life is being threatened by his ene-
mies, but, unknown to him, he is about to hear the signal
that reveals that he has been chosen Holy Roman
Emperor. In overwhelming sadness at the direction his
life has taken, he sings:

> Scepters! Riches! Honors! Beauties!
> Youth! What are you?
> Barks floating upon the sea of the years,
> which waves strike with constant troubles,
> until reaching the tomb's reef, your name
> plunges with you to nothingness!
> Oh, dreams and lying forms
> of my youthful years,
> if I believed in you too much,
> the spell now has vanished.[1]

In his youth Don Carlos had harbored false dreams and
illusions, illusions that life could bring unending happi-
ness and fulfillment, dreams that relationships would
last forever. Now, about to receive glory rather than

death, he finds wisdom, wisdom that brings with it compassion for his adversaries and strength to rule his people.

While cleverness and intelligence may accompany youth, wisdom is usually associated with those of mature years. This is, of course, not universally true. The Bible, which often makes the association of wisdom and age, recognizes the tragedy of age without wisdom and the possibility of wisdom in one who is young. "Better," declares the author of Ecclesiastes, "is a poor and wise youth than an old and foolish king" (Ecclesiastes 4:13). This truth is well illustrated in the Apocryphal book of Susanna and the Elders, in which the two lecherous elders are exposed by the wise intervention of the young Daniel. Shakespeare in *King Lear,* as if taking his text from the passage in Ecclesiastes cited above, exposes the tragedy of one who has become foolish in his old age. The aging monarch accepts the flattering but false words of his two daughters Goneril and Regan while rejecting the honest confession of the youngest, Cordelia. By so doing, he brings tragedy on himself and his entire household. The wisdom of age should have made Lear skeptical of flattery and aware that past actions are far more reliable guides to future behavior than easy assurances of undying love. Foolishness, however, prevails over wisdom, and death and sorrow ensue.

While wisdom does not come automatically with old age, wisdom seldom comes without the honing of life that long experience brings. Don Carlos' youthful illusions are like the illusions most of us held in our early years when life seemed simple, judgments black and white, goals obtainable by sincerity and hard work, relationships good or bad and relatively permanent. At some point, however, we discovered that some things are forever unobtainable, that despite the best intentions and heroic efforts love and friendship do not always last, that good intentions are not always rewarded, that even good and religious people can disappoint and betray us. Wisdom is not just disillusionment with youthful values and aspirations; wisdom requires that we move beyond the limited perspectives of your youthful experience in order to see life in its larger perspective and wholeness. Wisdom and age do not increase in direct proportion to one another, but wisdom usually requires a good measure of life experience for its growth.

Wisdom also cannot be equated with accumulated information, or with the ability to produce beautiful works in music, sewing, carpentry, painting, or other creative fields, or even with the ability to do research and come up with new insights or new theoretical constructs. Wisdom is not something we attain by our strenuous efforts or our high intelligence. Wisdom may have been transmitted to us in a variety of ways, but it is fundamentally a gift of God. This does not mean that wisdom is exclusively manifest in religious people. Elements of wisdom and foolishness appear in both religious and nonreligious people, and the Bible is quite open about this fact. But in both the synagogue and the early church, wisdom is associated with age. The term of honor given to leaders is that of "elder." It is from the Greek word for elder that we derive our words "presbyter" and "priest."

But what is wisdom? What does it mean to be wise? I asked this question in a class on "Ministry With and To Older People," a class of fourteen seminary students and twelve people in their sixties and seventies.

I asked them to picture someone they know who is both old and wise, to talk with another person about the qualities they see in that wise man or woman, and then to share their observations. After that sharing and some discussion, we agreed upon the following list of qualities of our wise acquaintances:

1. They are still learning, open to change and new ideas.
2. They have had a great variety of experiences and are able to put them together.
3. They are secure enough in themselves to accept others despite differences of opinion or behavior.
4. They recognize their limitations and are comfortable in letting others know about them.
5. They are able to look forward to tomorrow rather than fear it.
6. They are able to see the positive side of things.
7. They know themselves and can communicate who they are to others.
8. They have the capacity to give to others.
9. They have an indefinable "something" which lets you go in to see them feeling "down" and to come out feeling "up."
10. They have the ability to be "with" other people, to have empathy.
11. They take care of themselves.
12. They have a wholistic approach to life.

13. They have a sense of humor, "a twinkle in their eyes."

This is only the product of twenty-six people engaging in a fifty-minute exercise, but it helps focus on three important qualities of wisdom. The first is that wisdom involves one's total orientation to life rather than the accumulation of specific knowledge or skills. Those of us who have spent years acquiring graduate degrees are not excluded from among the wise, but we do not necessarily have an advantage over our less learned peers. One of the people cited by the class members dropped out of school after the eighth grade but is still learning at eighty-four. Wise people, it appears, have an openness to life that permits continued growth and continued appreciation of the new and the old, the familiar and the unfamiliar.

The second quality of wisdom my class members recognized is evidenced in the way we relate to others. Our wise elders had the ability "to give to others," "to have empathy," and "to accept others despite differences of opinion or behavior." This quality of wisdom was seen by both older and younger students as stemming from self-acceptance. As we accept ourselves, we are enabled to accept others. As we learn to love ourselves, we are freed to love others. One man in my class described his wife as a person who had grown wise with age. After joking about her ability to accept him and his "bad habits" through their fifty-two years of marriage, he became serious as he attributed her wisdom to her life in the church and years of volunteer work in her denominational home for the aged. She had grown wise through giving of herself to others. It would appear not only that wisdom enables us to relate well to others, but that such relating and giving can in turn contribute to our growth in wisdom.

The third quality of wisdom identified by my class members is the ability to deal with the limits of life, either through faith acceptance or through humor. People who are wise know that their lives, their understanding, their years are limited. At times, the awareness of these limits may bring discouragement and despair, but, on the whole, wise people have learned to accept and even laugh at their limits. One octogenarian I met through a class member was a white-water canoeist when he was in his twenties. As he became older, he told me, he switched to sailing on Lake Michigan. As he moved past middle age, he traded his sailboat for a power boat. "And now?" I asked. "Now," he responded with a smile, "I enjoy walking on the beach!"

Ego Integrity Versus Despair

One approach to our understanding of the nature of wisdom comes to us through the work of Erik Erikson. Erikson affirmed an important spiritual as well as psychological truth when he identified the task of the final stage of life as striking a balance between "ego integrity and despair."[2] He described this task as that of coming to terms with "one's one and only life cycle." In this stage we develop wisdom—the wisdom of perceiving our lives as whole and with wholeness, despite the brokenness we share with all other persons. The tension between ego integrity and despair is never fully resolved in this life, but the balance for the person of wisdom is on the side of integrity, wholeness.

Ego integrity versus despair, however, is a complex state that incorporates other life tensions, especially—but not uniquely—for the religious individual. Among the tensions are these: (1) between owning one's life and the recognition that we own nothing; (2) between seeing one's life as continuously interdependent upon the lives of others and as isolated, alone; (3) between grieving the increasing losses which accompany aging and trusting that these losses are redeemed and restored in the God who is the source and ground of all being.

Owning One's Life and Recognizing
That We Own Nothing

No matter what our views may be of life after death (unless we are convinced by claims of reincarnation), wisdom invites us to accept the life we are now leading, the life that began with our birth and will end with our death, as the one earthly life we have to live. We need to accept the burden and responsibility of our individual selves. Despite the exigencies of fate, the fortunes of my unique hereditary and environmental influences, my life is *my* responsibility and no one else's. One of the more difficult persons for pastors or counselors to help is the one who claims to be an innocent victim of others or of the fates. During the months in which this chapter was taking form, I was in the process of recovering from a broken ankle and other injuries received in an automobile accident. One of the things that disturbed me about my temporarily disabled state was the effect of my dependency on my approach to life. I became dependent upon doctors, nurses, physical therapists, porters with wheel chairs in airports. It was a life stance which was both depressing and seductive to me: depressing because of the loss of power over my own life and activities and seductive because I found that I could fall into a pattern of relinquishing my personal responsibilities to others. After all, "What do you expect of a man with a broken ankle?" If I had not, somehow, been given the wisdom to meet as many of my commitments as I could manage, the time might have been even more difficult than it was, and I might have been an even more difficult patient! We need to own our own lives and relationships and the consequences of our choices and actions.

In tension with the necessary ownership of our own lives, however, is our recognition that we own nothing, and that we are simply stewards of our lives, our goods, and our relationships. One of the most beautiful chapels in the cathedral of Roskilde, the burial place of Danish monarchs, is the fifteenth-century chapel of Christian I. He and his Queen Dorothea are buried beneath simple slabs bearing their names. King Christian assumed that the chapel itself, a place for visitors to pray for, among other things, the repose of the monarchs' souls, was a sufficient memorial. The slabs, however, are now all but obscured by two immense alabaster and marble monuments bearing the carved images of two of Christian's descendants. In visiting this chapel I felt appreciation for the wisdom of a king who knew his limits, who knew that he, like all other people, was "from dust," and to dust he would return. I also felt amusement at the successors who spoiled the effect of the chapel with their ostentatious attempts to memorialize themselves with costly and elaborate tombs. To be sure, who among us has not felt the temptation to leave behind a monument or two to remind others of how great or good or at least how well intentioned we were? Who among us has the wisdom to be content with the simple slab acknowledging that we are as nothing before the grandeur of the Creator?

It is not just the temptation to believe that our ownership lasts beyond death that blocks our acquisition of wisdom. It is also the belief that even in this life we actually possess anything. One of the failings of our Western materialistic culture is our emphasis upon possessing things. The shopping center has become the center of American life, and we often acquire things in order to "kill time," not realizing that time can not be stopped or set back or reversed by our "getting and spending." I was recently struck by sadness as I joined a crowd of people pawing through goods at a garage sale, worldly goods being disposed of by the children after the death of their mother. "Getting and spending we lay waste our powers. . . ."

Our acquisition of possessions is not limited to objects. It also includes people. Let me first say that I believe that human relationships, our close and intimate ties with friends and loved ones, are of the very essence of life. It is no accident that Jesus virtually equated neighbor love and love of God. To act, however, as if we possessed other persons—whether they be our friends, our children, our parents, or our spouses—is very different from love. A basic understanding of Christian stewardship is that we are set in this world as caretakers, as stewards, not as possessors. When we fall into the error of believing that we possess another person, our relationship becomes poisoned by a kind of idolatry in which we substitute ourselves for the One who alone possesses anything or anyone.

Wisdom, then, is putting aside the foolishness of believing that we possess anything, especially other persons. In a positive vein, it is coming to accept mortality in ourselves and others. It is coming to accept, at least in part or in some small beginning way, that for all the loving communion that may happen between myself and another, we are separate beings. What happens to that person may cause me pain and grief and shake the equilibrium of my life, but we ultimately belong not to each other but to the One in whom we "live and move and have our being."

To be wise, is, in one sense, to be a good steward. The gospel story of the talents constitutes a plea for us to use what has been entrusted to us, but it is grounded in the truth that we own nothing, not even our lives.

Seeing One's Life as Interdependent on Others and as Isolated

Our lives are continuously interdependent upon the lives of others and yet also isolated, alone. What we do affects others and what they do affects us. We, indeed, "do not live to ourselves" nor "do we die to ourselves" (Rom. 14:7). Both our living and dying are "to the Lord," as St. Paul observes. Our living and dying are also within a complex network of relationships and within a personal, family, and community history. The story of who I am includes the story of a host of other persons. It is a story I cannot tell without telling about them and about our interrelatedness, our shared joys and sorrows, our gains and losses, our hope and despair. To be wise is to know ourselves in our interdependence on others—others both living and dead. What I do or decide affects them, and in turn their actions affect my life, for good or ill.

Our dependence on others is illustrated by a story in the Talmud, a story about a traveler who saw a man planting a carob tree. The traveler asks the planter:

How long does it take [for this tree] to bear fruit? The man replied: "Seventy years." He then further asked him: "Are you certain that you will live another seventy years?" The man replied: "I found [ready grown] carob trees in the world; as my forefathers planted them for me so I too plant these for my children."[3]

The storyteller then fell into a deep sleep for seventy years. When he awoke, he saw a man gathering the fruit of the carob tree and he asked him, "Are you the man who planted the tree?" The man replied: "I am his grandson." We are debtors to our parents and grandparents for the trees from which we pick fruit, for the cities in which we live, for the art and literature and music we enjoy, for the discoveries that enrich our lives. In turn, we pass on to our heirs the fruit of our labor and imagination. Our lives are dependent upon countless others, both those who have preceded us, and those among whom we live.

However, wisdom recognizes another truth, in tension with the truth about our interdependence: the truth that we are alone, separated from all others. No one can experience what we are experiencing in physical pain or pleasure, in emotional euphoria or agony. No one can live or die for us. In one sense, our life and death are solitary matters, and it is presumptuous for me or anyone else to say to you, "I know how you feel." It is wisdom to know that we are solitary, isolated individuals. It is a further step toward wisdom to be at some measure of peace with our aloneness, to know that not only can we live with that fearful truth, but that only in doing so can we discover at least one aspect of the truth of our unique being.

Grieving the Increasing Losses Accompanying Aging and Trusting that These Losses Are Redeemed and Restored by God

Grieving is an essential part of life. The work of grief grows with age because of the increasing losses accompanying our aging. For many of us, this begins with the loss of the parents who bore and nurtured us and now leave us to be the older generation. Freud observed that the most important day in a man's life is the day his father dies. The same could be said of a woman in regard to her mother. This is not to minimize earlier childhood losses of friends and pets, familiar neighborhoods, and beloved teachers. We begin the grieving process early in life, perhaps as early as the day we give up our mother's breasts for other less personal sources of sustenance. The loss of parents, however, marks for most of us the beginning of a series of losses for which we must grieve and through grief learn to surrender what we once held close but have now lost.

In tension with grief is another stance towards life and its inevitable losses, the stance of trust or faith of believing that this loss is somehow redeemed in and by the God who is the source and ground of all people and things. We cannot, however, speak the word of faith lightly or glibly. Trusting and grieving are not alternative ways of reacting to loss, but are in tension, in coexistence with one another. To ask one in grief to exchange tears for faith is damaging and foolish advice. The men and women I know who have had the most difficulty in coming to terms with loss have usually been those who, because they mistakenly believed it to be right or virtuous, have denied their grief and put on a mantle of premature faith, saying such glib and pious words as, "It's no sense grieving. After all, we know that she is safe and with the Lord." At the right time, of course, these words are blessed words of faith, but at too early a time, as an escape from the necessary work of grief, they are harmful and diminish the wholeness that is wisdom.

The tension between grieving over our losses and accepting them in faith is illustrated in the novel *Flood*, by Robert Penn Warren. He develops his plot around a river town in Tennessee that is about to be inundated by the waters rising behind a newly constructed dam. The Baptist preacher, himself dying from cancer, plans a final service in his church that will both celebrate the death of their town and affirm that despite this death their individual and corporate lives have been blessed. The wisdom Brother Potts expresses is part of the wisdom of the aged, the wisdom to grieve our losses while trusting that they are in some strange way blessed, redeemed by God. The simple hymn Warren causes the preacher to compose affirms:

When I see the town I love
  Sinking down beneath the wave,
God, help me to remember then
  All the blessings that You gave.

When I see the life I led
  Whelmed and sunk beneath the flood,
Let the waters drown regret and envy—
  Make me see my life was good.[4]

The Gift to Be Shared

I began this chapter with a story about one king. I shall close with a story of another. Shortly after Solomon became king, we are told, God spoke to him in a dream and offered him a favor, saying, "Ask what I shall give you" (1 Kings 3:5). Solomon, instead of asking for riches or power or honor, asked for wisdom. God, pleased at this choice, bestowed upon Solomon this gift and all the others as well. Solomon's choice pleased God because wisdom is a gift to be used for the well-being of others. Wisdom, while it is a precious gift to the individual, is always a gift to be shared, a light that cannot be "hidden under a bushel" but must be set forth for the good and enlightenment of others. It is conveyed, however, not as a truth to be forced on others, but as a truth to which one must witness.

The inner imperative of wisdom is that it is to be communicated to others rather than to be kept and savored for one's self. Matthew Fox in his book *A Spirituality Named Compassion*[5] claims that there are at least two models of spirituality. The first of these he

76

refers to as "Climbing Jacob's Ladder," a model that emphasizes the solitary quest for enlightement, a quest that tends to isolate the searcher and engages the person in a competitive struggle to be higher and better. Fox, however, sees another model, one he calls "Dancing Sarah's Circle." This model is a corporate venture which draws us into face-to-face, hand-to-hand relationship with others, a relationship in which celebration replaces climbing and in which interdependence replaces ruthless independence. Spirituality that draws men and women together in a sharing quest heightens their compassion, their sense of the oneness of men and women everywhere. The fruit of this spirituality is wisdom, a wisdom that incorporates the threefold movement of love: toward God, toward neighbor, toward one's self.

Notes

1. *Ernani,* music by Guiseppe Verdi, libretto by Francesco Maria Piave (based on Victor Hugo's *Hernani*), literal translation by William Weaver, (New York: R.C.A., 1968).
2. Erikson, Erik H., *Childhood and Society* (New York: W. W. Norton and Company, Inc., 1963), p. 274.
3. *The Babylonian Talmud, Seder Mo'Ed,* vol. 4, translated under the editorship of Rabbi Dr. I. Epstein (London: Soncino Press, 1938).
4. Warren, Robert Penn, *Flood* (New York: Random House, 1963), pp. 239 and 438.
5. Fox, Matthew, *A Spirituality Named Compassion* (Minneapolis: Winston Press, 1979), pp. 36-67.

Intergenerational Relationships: Adult Children and Aging Parents
Helen Kandel Hyman

The elderly do not live in a separate world of their own. Old age is not a sealed vacuum, impervious to outside influences. For better or for worse, the lives of the older generations are intertwined, often closely, with the lives of the younger generations. Like pebbles dropping into still waters, the fortunes—both good and bad—of older relatives send ripples down the years that touch and often strongly influence the lives of children, grandchildren, and even great-grandchildren. The younger generations send out ripples of their own, which in turn affect the lives of the older ones.

There is nothing new in this intergenerational involvement. It has been going on since the world began. Remember the story of Ruth and Naomi? The difference today is in scale—in numbers. In the past, few people lived to be old, so intergenerational relationships were fewer and lasted, with rare exceptions, for less time. Average life-expectancy was eighteen in ancient Greece, thirty-three in the year 1600 and forty-seven when the twentieth century began. Today in the United States it is over seventy-three. As Ronald Blythe points out in *A View From Winter*:

If a Renaissance . . . man could return he would be as much astonished by the sight of two or three thousand septuagenarians and octogenarians lining a South Coast on a summer's day . . . as he would be by a television set. His was a world where it was the exception to go gray, to reach menopause, to become senile.

There are more than twenty-four million people over age sixty-five in the United States—more than 12 percent of the population. Predictions indicate that this number may rise to 25 percent at some point after the dawn of the twenty-first century. Earlier in this century few children grew to adulthood with living grandparents. Many of today's children will grow up not only knowing grandparents, but great-grandparents and even great-great-grandparents. Three-and four-generation families are seen frequently and the five-generation family is no longer uncommon. According to Dr. Robert Butler, former director of the National Institute on Aging, "This is the century not only of old age but of multi-generational families."

The family itself has undergone changes, particularly in the second half of this century. With the prevalence of divorce and remarriage, the family has enlarged its network with a proliferation of step-relationships. Today's children may have not only step-parents and step-siblings, but step-grandparents as well. So the ripples caused by elderly relatives are sending out ever-widening circles.

Until recently the involvement of families with their elderly members went unrecognized or unnoticed. As a matter of fact, the subject of old age in general was nearly taboo, especially in the period of the Youth Culture in the 1960s and 1970s. The emphasis was then on being young, acting young, feeling young. The families of the elderly struggled along for themselves when problems arose, trying to cope as best they could. Occasionally there was talk of the "nuclear" family—mother, father, children—living egocentric lives, exclusive, self-contained units sharing little and caring less about the older generations. This accusation was and still is justified for some families, but certainly not for the majority.

Gerontologists recognize that in spite of today's changing patterns the family plays a central role in the support system of its elderly relatives. Community services and programs, originally developed for the aging population, are now also designed to assist, extend, and relieve the ongoing care provided by younger family members. The old familiar accusation that "young people these days just don't care about their old parents" cannot be used broadside. More than three-quarters of the twenty-four million people over sixty-five have at least one living child. According to a sample survey aging parents and their children usually maintain ongoing contact with each other. Eighty-five percent of the parents with living children have at least one child living less than an hour away. Sixty-six percent saw one child the very day they were interviewed and only 2 percent had not seen any of their children within the past year.

The family is acknowledged as playing a crucial role in the lives of its elderly members, and sons and daughters try to perform their roles well, yet may of them still feel that they are not doing enough. As hard as they try, they still feel guilty about the perceived inadequacy of their efforts, suffering periodic unease that "we are not caring enough for those who cared for us." The classic guilt-raiser, "One mother can take care of ten children but ten children cannot take care of one old mother," strikes home to many. The younger generation, trying to juggle a variety of conflicting responsibilities, may even feel that King Lear was pointing directly to them when he wailed, "How sharper than a serpent's tooth it is to have a thankless child."

Who are all these "thankless children"? They are the middle generations sandwiched between the older and the younger, pulled in opposing directions by stresses on either side. They are found in every part of the country and at every economic level. Some of them are young parents rearing young children, building careers and at the same time trying not to neglect their aging parents. "Do I get the sitter for the children so I can be with Father? Or do I get the sitter for Father so I can be with the children?" sighs a young mother. "Can I accept a promotion a thousand miles away? If I do, I'll be leaving my old parents behind. How will they manage? But what about my own career?" worries a young father.

Another group of thankless children are in their forties and fifties. They have no youngsters around any more and fewer domestic responsibilities. Life should be easier for them by now, but perhaps it is not. Perhaps they are facing the high cost of college tuition for their adolescent children and working harder to pay the bills. Perhaps they are at peak career with demanding jobs or —conversely—experiencing career setbacks, lack of advancement, financial reverses, even unemployment or layoffs. Perhaps the women are now back to work again —and enjoying it—after years of domestic routine. Perhaps husbands and wives are seeing their own old age coming closer or experiencing some of the diffuse bewildering symptoms of menopause, male and female.

And then there is a third group—men and women in their sixties and seventies, still concerned about parents in their eighties and nineties. These older sons and daughters are already in the senior class themselves, many of them grandparents by now. They are looking squarely at their own aging, perhaps with diminished health, stamina, and resources. They may be coping with their own retirement and reduced incomes. They may even be widowed by now. What if their children and their grandchildren still need help? How can there be enough physical, financial, or emotional strength to go around, to share with other family members equally?

There is more help for these middle generations today than there was a few decades ago. Starting in the 1970s, old age, once taboo, has become quite a favored subject in the popular media. The public has become more familiar with the variety of supportive services available in many communities. Instead of trying to solve all their problems themselves, people have discovered there is help to be found when elderly relatives develop problems. Nonprofessional people can often talk quite knowledgeably about nursing homes, daycare centers, meals on wheels, transportation services, Social Security, Medicare and Medicaid.

Even though such community services are around, many families are still reluctant to turn to them, feeling that if they do they will be breaking the commandment to "honor your father and your mother." "If I let someone else help my parents, it will look as though I don't love them enough," one such reluctant daughter may say. Or "People will think I'm not a good daughter." Why should this be true? Is love simply chauffeuring and housecleaning and cooking and nursing? Often it is harder for children to show their love when they let themselves become overburdened with extra responsibilities. An aging mother might discover that if outsiders help with her domestic routines there will be more time for pleasure and real companionship with her children. Perhaps she'll have a chance to talk more about her feelings, worries, and fears, and perhaps her children will be freer to listen.

When families are willing to ask for outside help they may find to their dismay that not much exists in their communities or that it is prohibitively expensive. Too little is reimbursable under Medicare or not enough is allowed by Medicaid. If outside services do exist, one person is needed to act as general coordinator, making sure that the help an elderly parent needs flows constantly and does not break down. This caretaker role has been traditionally taken by daughters, most frequently by one particular daughter. She either assumes the role voluntarily or is assigned it by her parents or brothers and sisters. When there is no daughter to act as caretaker, especially when extensive or intensive care is needed, nursing home placement may become necessary. The daughter's role in the care of the elderly is considered so crucial that one gerontologist claims that the words "alternatives to institutionalization" are merely a euphemism for the word "daughters." Sometimes these daughters are over sixty-five themselves.

In any discussion of relationships between older and younger generations, there is always the danger that problems will be emphasized and benefits ignored. Tolstoi wrote in *Anna Karenina*, "All happy families resemble one another. Every unhappy family is unhappy in its own fashion." There is a tendency to focus on the various "fashions" of difficulties that arise for the elderly and affect their families. But the benefits derived from warm intergenerational relationships must never be ignored. They are unique in our experience of life and may offer treasures to be found nowhere else.

The fact that parents and grandparents are growing older does not necessarily mean that they will ever turn to their families for anything except companionship and pleasure. Millions of older people continue right on into their seventies and eighties—even into their nineties— firmly in control of their own lives and often still firmly controlling their children's lives, too. They may still pursue their own interests and routines, handle their own finances, make their own decisions, and probably resent interference. Old age of itself is not a problem, nor does it inevitably produce problems or dependency.

Countless stories can be told of gratifying relationships between the generations with love and mutual enjoyment, as well as concrete help, flowing as much from the older to the younger as from the younger to the older. The generations mix and mingle, each one living independently but drawing strength and support from the other. Vigorous, independent, self-sufficient octogenarians are not only splendid sources of enjoyment, wisdom, and advice for their children and grandchildren, but they can be comforting role models, too. Their very satisfactory existence can prove to younger people that growing old is not so terrible after all. Old age and the aging process are still shrouded in misconceptions and false assumptions. No wonder men and women approach their own aging with fear and dread.

Look at the most familiar misconceptions that are widely held: to be old is to be sick, lonely, poor, useless, finished, sexless. These descriptions do fit some of the nation's elderly, but they can be applied to many younger people, too. They certainly cannot be applied to all the elderly. Every day millions are proving these myths false by continuing to function productively right on to the end. The myth that to be old is to be sick can be refuted by fact and figure. Of the more than twenty-four million elderly, only 15 percent are unable to carry on normal activities. The elderly population average less than fifteen days a year in bed because of illness. And finally, for those who believe that old people usually end up in nursing homes, only 5 percent of the elderly are in institutions at any one time.

One of the most serious causes of misunderstanding is that catchall phrase "sixty-five-and-older," which is used to describe senior citizens. More and more people are living into the later decades. Our total population has increased threefold since 1900, but the elderly segment has increased fivefold. The group over eighty-five is the fastest growing segment of the population. So when we blithely talk of the nation's senior citizens, we may be talking of a range of thirty years. A daughter of seventy-two may be caring for a mother of ninety-five, yet both these women are included in that crude category.

The sixty-fifth birthday is not a magical date when people plunge headlong into old age as if into a swimming pool. Yet this label is placed on twenty-four million individuals who have an infinite variety of individual interests, life-styles, personalities, problems, and physical ailments. There are the sick and the healthy, the introverts and the extroverts, the productive and the inactive, the joiners and the loners, just as there are at any other stage in the life cycle. People over sixty-five are eligible for Medicare or Medicaid; they can draw pensions and collect Social Security. But these are the only things they all have in common with each other.

Look at the first three decades of life and the changes that thirty years can bring. Clear stages are recognized: infancy, childhood, adolescence, maturity. But the last thirty years are lumped together in a single category. Professionals are trying to make more sense out of these years by referring to the young-old—65-74, the middle-aged old—75-84, and the old-old—85 and up. Health problems and needs are different for each of these stages. A condition that is an inconvenience for someone who is young-old may become a difficult handicap for the same person at middle-aged old and possibly an incapacitating problem at the old-old stage. For example, poor vision may one day turn into blindness, diabetes may progress until amputation is necessary, arthritis may become totally crippling.

It is unfair, however, to be too critical of the fact that the final thirty years have not been more realistically described. These years are confusing because the aging process is so unpredictable. It moves at different rates for different people. It is known within a certain range when children will walk, talk, go through puberty. But there is no such predictability in the aging process, even for brothers and sisters in the same family. Every individual suffers a certain amount of physical loss as the years go by. This goes on visibly as skin and hair change and invisibly within the body. But there is no predicting when these losses will take place or when, if ever, the losses will become serious handicaps. The recuperative powers of two patients of the same age recovering from the same serious illness can vary tremendously. One may return to autonomous living in a matter of weeks while the other retires into permanent invalidism. For this reason it is difficult for the families and for the elderly themselves to see into the future and to figure out how much care will be needed and for how long. Personality and emotions play a crucial role, too, complicating things even further.

Frank Wilson and his younger sister, Mary, were both in their eighties and both suffered from seriously impaired vision. Frank, a determined and indomitable character, managed somehow despite his semi-blindness to live alone, take care of himself, even to travel. He read the newspaper every day with a complicated contraption he had rigged up for himself consisting of a green eyeshade, a high intensity light and a rolled up tube of paper through which he sighted with one eye on the print. His sister, with the same degree of impairment and several years younger, gave up before she was eighty, referred to herself as blind, and become completely dependent on her overburdened younger daughter.

Another prevailing false assumption is that independence is an all-or-nothing situation for the elderly. When widowed Gilbert Cuseo had a stroke in his mid-seventies, his children were frantic while he was recuperating in the hospital. "Father can't live alone any more! He'll have to go to a nursing home or come to live with one of us! But which one of us can take him?" Luckily his children were in such a turmoil that they were unable to make any decision. In the meantime old Mr. Cuseo surprised everyone by making an almost complete recovery. Families often assume the worst and see nothing but disaster ahead when an aging parent suffers a stroke, or a heart attack, or when doctors discover dreaded symptoms of cancer, glaucoma, diabetes. But such panic is often premature. The road to the nursing home is a long one with many detours and stopovers along the way. Remember that at any given time only 5 percent of the elderly are in nursing homes. And contrary to what many sons and daughters assume, most parents do not want to live with their children but prefer to remain independent as long as possible—ideally forever.

Even if total independence cannot continue forever, some portion of it can usually be maintained. Except in sudden tragic instances—a massive stroke, a major heart attack, a serious accident—people do not usually go from total independence to total dependence overnight. Independence usually dwindles slowly away.

After an acute illness or with the slow progression of some chronic physical condition, an elderly man may lose some portion of his ability to manage independently. He may need help in that area of his life which has become weak, but he may be as strong as ever in other areas. If he can find the necessary support, he may still be able to continue living independently. "A good daughter is the one who takes care of her aging father" may have once been considered a fine definition of filial devotion. But a better definition today might be "A good daughter is the one who helps her aging father take care of himself."

Care for the elderly may be described as having three levels of intensity. The lowest level can be called *on-and-off care*. It is not continual and not intense. Help may be needed only during special periods related to a minor illness, a depressive episode, recovery from a fall. Temporary care of this kind may be especially support-ive following a bereavement, the death of a husband, a wife, a child. It is also essential during a posthospital convalescence.

Eighty-seven-year-old Sandra Rose, who lived alone in an apartment complex for the elderly, recently had a double cataract operation. After a brief hospital stay she returned to her own apartment and was willing to have a homemaker, hired by her daughter, come in four hours a day. But as she told her daughter soon afterwards, "I get my new glasses on Thursday and then, thank God, that woman goes!" Once she felt able to manage alone she was impatient to have her on-and-off care turned off for good—or at least until she needed it again.

Ongoing supportive care is a middle-range level needed by older people whose disabilities have perma-nently limited their functioning in some areas but not in others. They are not likely to improve, but they are able to get along well enough if they have continuing support in their weak areas. Supportive ongoing care may be required by older people who are severely arthritic, par-tially blind, or partially paralyzed, as well as by those who have no special infirmity but are generally weakening. It is also needed by those who are physcially sound but mentally impaired.

And finally, there is *long-term intensive care* for the chronically and seriously ill or disabled. It is only at this point that independence finally dwindles away. This level of care is the most demanding, the most difficult to provide, and the most disastrously expensive. All three levels of care can be provided by a support system of relatives, friends, and community services, although when long-term intensive care becomes too burdensome, nursing home placement may be the only solution.

The independence so treasured by the elderly can be jeopardized by devoted children even when there are no crises requiring some level of care. Mindful of the commandment to "honor your father and your mother," and anxious to see themselves or be seen by others as "good children," some sons and daughters may never realize that too much caring can be as harmful as too little. A daughter who rushes in at the first sign of faltering to "take over" for dear old Mom and Dad may seen to show admirable filial devotion. She may never dream that this devotion may weaken still further the old couple's faltering sense of self-reliance and self-esteem, making them become prematurely dependent. When children assume too much responsibility and make unilateral decisions according to their own rather than their parents' wishes, they become benign dictators. Such children would be surprised to learn that they may actually be killing their parents with kindness.

Kindness and devotion are sterling qualities. Many an elderly man or woman would welcome a small amount of both, but these qualities are more likely to produce successful results when accompanied by a genuine understanding of each individual's wishes, personality, and preferred life-style. The efforts of well-meaning children to provide "the kind of life *we* want for Mom and Dad" would probably succeed better if they encouraged instead "the kind of life Mom and Dad want for *themselves*." Look at these examples of benign dictatorship:

- Forcing Dad to retire because of his heart condition, to take it easy and enjoy himself at last. To some fathers, retirement is tantamount to dying.
- Bringing Mom from the run-down, dangerous urban neighborhood where she has lived for fifty years to the security and comfort of a pleasant suburb. Her family may feel greatly relieved that she is finally safe, but the alien surroundings may trigger a severe depression in a bewildered, confused Mom.
- Repeatedly reassuring Mom and Dad with the statement, "You must relax. We'll take care of everything." Everything may include driving the car, cooking meals, planning a vacation, choosing a doctor, making decisions. Such kind reassurance can boomerang. The message Mom and Dad receive is thay they are no longer capable of taking care of *anything*.

The most successful decisions are likely to be those arrived at jointly by everyone, with the elderly stating their preferences and the young offering suggestions and warnings.

Shortly after Katherine Prazer was widowed at seventy-nine, she announced that she was putting her house on the market and moving from Ohio to Florida to be near her old friend, Jenny. Her children knew that she and their father had been contemplating this move before he died, but they were worried that she was taking such a radical step alone and too quickly after she was widowed. They understood why she needed to get away from the old house so full of memories and didn't try to dissuade her. But they did suggest a compromise plan and urged her to make a temporary rather than a permanent move. "Why not rent the house for a year and see how things go in Florida?" her son suggested. "You may not like it there." Her daughter added, "You may not even like Jenny." Katherine accepted the compromise and took off for Florida. Exactly a year later she was ready to move back into her old house. "Jenny's a bore!" she announced to her children. "All she does is talk about her health. And anyway, who wants to live in a place where it never snows?"

No discussion of intergenerational relationships can be complete without some reference to emotions, not only the feelings of the older and younger generations toward each other, but also feelings of younger people about old age in general and their parents' aging specifically. These feelings may seriously affect how they behave towards their parents. Those with a postive attitude toward growing old are more likely to be able to reach out to their elderly parents with concern and constructive support. But if old age is viewed with apprehension and dread—as it is by so many in today's society —a parent's aging can be very threatening. It forces younger people to contemplate their own old age and eventual death.

Feelings also intervene as families watch valued relatives, formerly sources of strength and comfort, begin to decline. A mother's hands shake. A father becomes forgetful or slightly disoriented. These well-loved people can no longer provide the support they once did. These changes are painful to see, but some children can accept them—although with great sadness and regret—realizing that their parents will not live forever. Others cannot contemplate losing the people they have always depended on and may react with fear or even anger. Or they may refuse to admit that anything is wrong, ignoring physical symptoms and complaints. A problem may be denied until it is too late for medical intervention that might alleviate or perhaps even reverse the frightening symptoms.

Perhaps the most crucial emotions are the tangled, mixed-up feelings between the generations. Here again, when emotions are positive, it is easier for children to remain close to their parents and be supportive when needed. When feelings are negative or conflicted, problems between the generations are likely to intensify.

Long-standing relationships between parents and children often determine how much contact there will be in later years and how much these children are willing or able to help when their parents grow old. These relationships have been thirty, forty, fifty years in the making. Some relationships modify, and the intensity may lessen when children grow up and move away from daily parental involvement; but life-time patterns are not easy to change. One daughter asks her widowed father to live with her and her family. Together they form a successful three-generation household. Her neighbor down the street cannot take this step. She loves her father, too, but differently. Her love is mixed with fear, or with a dependency he'd never let her outgrow, or with resentment that her older sister always was, and still is, his favorite. The way he treated her as a child may well determine how she is able to treat him when she is grown up and he is old. But the guilt she feels because she cannot do more for him can trigger another emotion, anger. She is angry with herself for not helping more and angry at him for making her feel guilty. She withdraws even further and when others provide whatever help is needed, feels guiltier yet.

Feelings also intervene when brothers and sisters try to work cooperatively with each other to provide the help their parents need. While these cooperative efforts produce wonders in some families, in others where there has always been tension and rivalry, these emotions are likely to flare up again and torpedo the best laid plans. Brothers and sisters often do not agree on a course to be followed, so a stalemate occurs. The ailing mother or father is forgotten, while old battles dating from the nursery are waged all over again. The favorite child and the less favored may keep on fighting for the prize "Mother loves me best," even when the children are in their sixties and Mother is over eighty. Mother may still fan the flames and play favorites from her wheelchair.

Some adults can face up to their feelings about their parents, or their brothers and sisters, and evaluate them honestly. Others are unaware of what they feel or, if aware, deny it to themselves and everyone else. An objective observer, a doctor, a minister, or a family therapist can often help family members sort out all these mixed-up feelings and learn to live with them. But strangely enough, even though they are in painful turmoil, many families seek out this kind of help only as a last resort. They may doggedly keep right on searching for the right nursing home, the right housing, the right homemaker, the right doctor—never realizing that their tangled emotions are preventing them from finding the right anything. When these emotions are faced honestly, they no longer get in the way of constructive action, and both generations are better off.

The commandment to "honor your father and your mother" does not offer specific guidelines as to how the honor should be provided. This is just as well, since no one pat formula can be applied. When it comes to intergenerational relationships, personalities and lifestyles of every close family member have to be taken into account. So do finances, job pressures, and health factors. Solutions that work for one family may not work for another and should probably not even be considered. As one young woman said recently, "I can't have Mother live with us. It just won't work. But we all want to help her and we are helping. Life's pretty good now for all of us—for Mother, my children, and for my husband and me. It's not perfect, but I don't really expect there is a perfect solution."

It would be comforting to most daughters and sons if they could have such realistic expectations. Then perhaps they would feel less guilt when things are imperfect. No matter how hard she tries, a daughter will never be able to make her parents young again. She may not even be able to make them happy again. She's never going to turn them back into the strong, supportive people they used to be. She's certainly not going to transform them into the parents she always wished she had—but never did. But if she sets her goals realistically, she *can* expect to find ways to make her parents' lives easier, more meaningful, more satisfying, less lonely, and generally more livable, without demanding too many sacrifices from her children, her husband, and herself. If she can accomplish this, then she and her parents will have more time to enjoy each other's company before it's too late.

Informal Support for Older Persons: A Role for Religious Organizations

Claudia B. Cluff and Leighton E. Cluff

The Need for Informal Support

An understanding of the spirituality of the older person must acknowledge and take seriously the significance of the human body. For our thinking and feeling about the world and God will express the way we think and feel about ourselves as bodies. Biological aging—changes in appearance, illness, or disability—can affect not only the human body but also the human spirit. Likewise, spiritual, emotional, and psychological poverty may exacerbate illness and disability. The physical and spiritual needs and concerns of people, young and old, are inextricably linked.

Precisely for this reason the provision of human support in caring for older persons is a substantial component of quality health care. Although technology can prevent, cure, or ameliorate many diseases and physical impairments, human support—including personal assistance, encouragement, and compassion—is important to restoring or improving functional effectiveness and meeting the ultimate goal of medical care: enhancing the quality of an individual's life.

Although some individuals are better able than others to cope and care for themselves, no one can deal with every adverse circumstance without help from others. There are many who can face acute, chronic, or terminal illness and senescence and remain not only functionally effective but become strengthened both personally and spiritually. Others facing similar problems may become depressed, withdrawn, bitter, and incapacitated. There are many gradations between these extremes, irrespective of the severity or nature of the impairment or disease. Nevertheless, the need for both medical care *and* human support remains indubitable.

During the past two decades, the need for supportive services has led to new programs and professions within the formal care system, including patient advocates or ombudsmen, health eductors, social workers, and nurses specialized in non-technologic aspects of care. Diverse community organizations have also developed as sources of aid. They include national organizations concerned with individual diseases; university programs in which students assist dependent people in the community; home health care groups that help with meals, housekeeping, or transportation; community programs to support victims of physical or substance abuse; and many other activities. Increasing appropriation of public funds beginning in the mid-sixties accelerated the movement to formalization and professionalization of supportive care services.

Although the expansion of these service programs was prompted by numerous factors, the fragmentation of traditional informal or natural supports had had a critical role in increasing the need for alternative care systems. The mobility of the population, economic factors, divorce and separation, and changes in social structures and values have all served to limit the effectiveness of informal systems of care, to sever individuals from sources of support, and magnify the role of formal programs and professionals in providing human support.

Formal support systems and professionals have assumed an important role in the health care delivery system, but the intermittent intervention of professionals cannot satisfactorially replace the perpetuity of interactions and the human support of family, friends, neighbors, or religious communities. Samaritanism or human support and technology are the cornerstones of medical practice. The physician's particular knowledge and skill for helping patients is in the use of medical technology, but technology alone often is insufficient in the absence of human support. Conversely, human support alone is insufficient when techonology can be used to make an individual's life better.

Complaints about medical care often converge on the conviction that today's doctors are less responsive to the personal or human needs of their patients. Measurement of the impact of human support upon a patient's well-being or functional effectiveness, however, has been difficult, in contrast to measurement of the effectiveness of technology in correcting disease or impairments.

There is not convincing evidence that education in the behavioral or social sciences prepare physicians to provide human support. Personal experiences with patients in their homes or community and observing physicians who give human support—which is rarely provided in training settings—probably are the most effective ways to develop or enhance the human support function of physicians.

Although patients in institutions such as hospitals and nursing homes are dependent upon others to administer and apply medical technology used in their care, they, too, are in need of human support that is beyond what is offered by health professionals. Natural or informal supports can help alleviate the isolation, loneliness, fear, and apprehension of patients in hospitals and nursing homes if physicians and other health professionals involve them in patient care, by helping them understand medical technology, what to expect, and how they can contribute to patients' needs. The support provided by others, and patients' personal responsibility for their own care, can be more effective when buttressed by a rational understanding of medicine and medical technology. Unfortunately, however, health professionals, who also need their own human support, may resent or fail to appreciate what can be offered to their patients by nonprofessionals.

Informal support is needed by anyone who is acutely or chronically ill and infirm, but especially by elderly persons. Disabled infants, children, and adults also need informal support, but the impaired elderly now are the largest and fastest growing population requiring such support.

Many disabled are maintained at home or in the community, and the severity of their disability alone does not mandate, nor is it always responsible for, institutionalization. Admission to nursing homes, for example, is not only because of the severity of disability. Ten to twenty percent of all persons in skilled nursing homes are placed in these institutions because they do not have the support they need in the community.

Economic limitations of individuals and families and public or government financial assistance for institutional care can militate against an infirm elderly person remaining in the home or community. A key factor, however, that determines whether or not a disabled individual remains at home or in the community is the availability of informal support provided by family, neighbors, and friends. This support is often pivotal in preventing institutionalization or the excessive and often unnecessary use of formal or professional services.

Although able to give informal support, families, neighbors, and friends may not be able to provide what is needed. When infirm or disabled persons receive less than optimal assistance, those who provide informal support can feel insecure, frustrated, and ineffective; this may lead to the institutionalization of the person for whom they are responsible.

Problems in Meeting the Need

Special retirement "communities," such as Continuing Care Retirement (Life Care) facilities, that attempt to provide informal support and formal health care services for elderly persons are attractive but too expensive for wide application. Furthermore, they usually require medical evidence of good health prior to admittance. Although residents of such "communities" may become infirm, those who are disabled often are not admitted.

Nursing homes are a poor substitute for human support. In many instances, nursing homes are unsatisfactory and expensive replacements for person-centered informal support in the home or community.

Congregate housing, foster home care, and residential apartments have been used for some people, serving as alternatives to institutionalization at least temporarily. No very effective mechanism has been established to provide the support needed for mentally ill or retarded persons who become deinstitutionalized. Group or sheltered housing has accommodated some of these people but probably has been unsatisfactory in providing much of the support and services many of then require. It seems unlikely that such arrangements will provide all the support needed by these individuals. Communities will have to develop other ways to provide the support so often required.

Hospices have used informal volunteers to provide support in the care of the dying and their families. As federal funding for hospice care increases, however, the support provided may become more professionalized and formalized and may thereby diminish the informal personal support that is needed by dying persons and their families.

Groups with common medical problems have helped their members gain better understanding, adhere to regimens of care, cope and adapt, and maintain or improve functional effectivenes. Many individuals with disabilities, however, do not belong to such groups and may have to deal with their problems alone and without the support of others.

Religious organizations or congregations have traditionally contributed to human support, are well suited to do so, and could assume a mediating role between formal care and persons in need. A few congregations have attempted to develop programs to meet the needs of infirm elderly people. Too often, however, the programs have lacked outreach to the community.

Few institutions, however, are more appropriately suited to respond to the human support needed by suffering people. Churches and synagogues exist in virtually every community, and they promote values of human belonging, family, and caring in our society. Their tradition is to respond to the needs of others, and this serves as the basis and motivation for voluntarism. Even when the nuclear family has been eroded, the religious community has often viewed itself as the extended family, providing for those in need a place where they can obtain human support. Because of the nature of the religious community and its programs, issues such as eligibility or restrictive guidelines are of little or no importance. No person is necessarily excluded from receiving assistance.

Churches and synagogues, therefore, are ideally suited to assume a mediating role between the formal care system and individuals and families in need. Too often, however, religious groups tend to be oriented centripetally rather than centrifugally and draw people into the church rather than reaching out into the community. Furthermore, as federal, state, and regional programs have been established, most religious congregations have not fully recognized nor developed their potential to provide personal support to those in the community who are in need and have too readily abrogated such responsibility. While there has been great resistance in establishing interfaith/ecumenical programs, parochialism also has hampered cooperative efforts even among neighboring churches of the same denomination. Churches and synagogues have also often been resistant in developing effective linkages with the formal agencies of care within their respective communities which are also important to those for whom the church might provide support.

Families and friends are central sources of informal support that have been generally ignored. Too little has been done to assist or enhance these natural supports. They need assistance in learning how to effectively provide support, and need support themselves in carrying out their responsibilities and fulfilling their role.

Methods of Solving the Problems

Those who provide informal support may have to know how to care for persons in bed or in wheelchairs, who require companionship and help in feeding or bathing or for persons who may be confused, disoriented, or hallucinating. "Nursing skills" can be taught by nurses, but many skills also can be taught by other caregivers or by organized groups of trained volunteers from the community. When such skills are not acquired, those who provide informal support often feel fearful and apprehensive, and may not be able to meet the needs of the disabled or infirm. Then their own lives can become ones of despair.

Churches, synagogues, and community organizations can serve an important "mediating role" in finding people who need help and recruiting those willing to provide support. They can develop ways to provide instruction and information for families and friends of those who need human support. They also can coordinate linkages with formal care systems to assure that they are integrated with informal caregivers in such a way that the needs of disabled and infirm persons are met most effectively.

It has yet to be determined, however, whether or not religious institutions and other community organizations will be committed to, accept, and fulfill such a mission.

Leisure and Learning:
A Spiritual Perspective

Nancy J. Osgood

"The aim of education is the wise use of leisure."

Aristotle

The United States has experienced nothing short of a demographic revolution during the nineteenth and twentieth centuries, resulting in what has been variously referred to as the maturing of our population and the "graying of America." Since 1900 the number and proportion of the population sixty-five and over have increased dramatically, from approximately three million (4 percent of the total population) in 1900, to twelve million in 1950, to twenty-six million today (11 percent of the total population).

People are living longer today than ever before in our nation's history. A child born in 1900 could expect to live approximately forty-five years, whereas a child born today can expect to live approximately seventy-four years (seventy-eight for females, seventy-one for males), almost doubling life expectancy. Life expectancy at age sixty-five has also increased. In 1900 it was just under twelve years; in 1980 it was sixteen years. Demographers refer to this situation as mass longevity. Never before in history have societies been faced with such numbers and proportions of older people.

Not only are more people living longer today than ever before, but they are also spending considerably more time outside of "productive" work in the labor force. In 1900 two-thirds of the males sixty-five and over were still employed, compared to 44.6 percent in 1955 and 19.9 percent in 1981 (U.S. Bureau of the Census, 1981).

Until very recently the problem with leisure was more finding it than deciding how to use it. Only after the institutionalization of retirement, which formally occurred in 1935 with the passage of the Social Security Act, did years of leisure become a reality for large numbers in our society. Today's elderly are a pioneer generation. They possess more free time, unconstrained by family and work obligations, than any other group of elderly in history and than any other age group in our present society. We can expect to live about one-third of our lives in leisure. Will this time be a burden or a blessing?

Already numerous critics have pointed to increased dehumanization, boredom, and meaninglessness in life as individuals sit idly in front of the television or engage in other such pursuits to fill their hours of free time. As so many individuals live so many years outside of productive employment, we need to ask, How can this abundant amount of leisure time be fulfilling? How can we harness the new leisure as a positive force and infuse the lives of those individuals over sixty-five with meaning?

Work has not always been exalted as the noblest of institutions. To the ancient Greeks, who forced slaves to do their work for them, work was nothing more than a curse. Leisure was the highest aim of life. The classical Greek and Roman philosophers conceived of leisure as something quite different from our modern-day concept of fun and games, tricky gadgets, and commercialized entertainment and amusements. The Greek word for leisure is *scholē*, from a verb that means "to halt" or "to cease," hence, "to have quiet or peace." The Latin verb *licere*, from which our English word leisure is derived, means "to be permitted" and the related noun, *license*, means "the absence of restraint or coercion" (Dahl 1972, 74). Thus the root meaning of the word "leisure" is freedom.

Composing and playing music, writing and reciting poetry, singing, fine conversation with worthy companions, and especially serene contemplation comprised the Greek view of leisure expressed in the term *scholē*. To the Greeks, leisure was the noblest of all activities, exemplifying the human aspect that was most godlike and that most distinguished humans from other animals. Work, on the other hand, was seen as brutalizing the mind, rendering one unfit to consider truth or to practice virtues.

The Greeks viewed leisure as an end in itself, with the highest order of pleasure being found in contemplation and celebration. For the Greeks leisure represented an attitude or state of mind and had no relation to clock time. Experiences were to be enjoyed for their own sake or their intrinsic value. The Roman Seneca stressed the unobligated character of leisure as its prime value, emphasizing the nobility of freedom. Socrates declared that "leisure is the best of all possessions." And Aristotle described leisure as the very basis of culture and center of life.

For the ancient Greeks contemplation, the highest form of leisure, was the way to Truth. The Greeks held that "spiritual and intellectual knowledge included an element of pure, receptive contemplation, or, as Heraclitus says, 'listening to the essence of things'" (Pieper 1952, 11). Epicurus similarly preached the quiet pleasures, "so that one could seek peace of the soul." Plato's academy was a religious association, as well as an academic association of intellectuals. Plato, Aristotle, and Epicurus all stressed serene contemplation, not only as a way to cultivate the mind and enhance creativity, but also as a means by which to gain spiritual knowledge and wisdom concerning God, the self, and life and as a way to enter a sense of deep rest, repose, and peace.

The history of Israel shows that religious life revolved around periods of abstinence from work. Holy days were frequent, and God's prohibitions against work were honored. Throughout the Old Testament we find prohibitions regarding work, especially on the sabbath and on designated feast days. Christ also taught that we do "not live by bread alone," that we are not to be anxious, for God will meet our needs:

Therefore I tell you, do not be anxious about your life, what you shall eat or what you shall drink, nor about your body, what you shall put on. Is not life more than food, and the body more than clothing? Look at the birds of the air: they neither sow nor reap nor gather into barns, and yet your heavenly Father feeds them. Are you not of more value than they? . . . Consider the lilies of the field, how they grow; they neither toil nor spin; yet I tell you, even Solomon in all his glory was not arrayed like one of these.

(Matthew 5:25-29 RSV)

Even God rested from the labor of creation on the seventh day, thus setting the example for rest from labor. The word sabbath is derived from the Hebrew root *shabhath*, which means "to cease," "to desist," "to rest." God sanctified the sabbath, and the third commandment is "Remember the sabbath, to keep it holy!"

God further set aside a sabbath year (Leviticus 25:2-7, 20-22; 26:34,43). Every seventh year the land was to lie fallow that it might enjoy a rest. No work was to be done that year; the people were to trust God to meet all their needs. Creditors were to cancel all debts, and servants were to be set free in the sabbath year. After seven sabbath years, on the fiftieth year the children of Israel were to enjoy a year of jubilee in which no work was to be done. God also set aside certain other holy days as special times for ritualistic festivity, contemplation, worship and adoration of God, and the expression of joy and celebration. They represented specially designated, God-given days of leisure.

Puritan teachings and the sermons and writings of Calvin, Luther, and the other Protestant leaders have not always been hospitable to leisure. "Idle hands are the Devil's workshop" and other stronger admonitions against leisure characterized the nineteenth century, referred to as the "golden age of work" (Tilgher 1930). In his writings, Calvin glorified work as a calling, and in the teachings of Calvin and Luther work became sanctified as a means of serving God.

In recent years various writers (Cox 1967, Keen 1970, Lee 1964, Moltmann 1972) developed a theology of play in which they emphasize the joy and celebration that accompany holy days and feasts. Pieper, in his important work *Leisure the Basis of Culture*, declares that "the soul of leisure lies in celebration." Dahl is another Christian writer who has recently examined leisure from a spiritual perspective, listing the ABCs of a Christian life of leisure: Abandon, Beauty, Celebration (Dahl 1972). The emphasis is on letting go and trusting God to meet daily needs, enjoying the beauty of nature, the arts, and life, and celebrating the gift of life and creation.

These modern-day religious philosophers treat leisure primarily as joy and celebration. But the sabbath and early holy days were also times set aside for contemplation. They were times in which to reflect on the meaning of God and the universe, moments to pause and ponder. Contemplation, meditation, quiet reflection, and prayer are proper forms of leisure. Contemplation implies a quiet receptiveness and openness in which we listen for the "still, small voice of the Spirit." Pieper's thesis is that leisure is not possible unless it has a durable and living link with the *cultus,* divine worship. In this sense leisure is viewed as a receptive attitude of mind, a state of serene contemplation, in which we "steep ourselves in the whole of creation and get in touch with ourselves and our Creator" (Pieper 1952, 28-29). Pieper's conception of leisure as contemplative celebration is reminiscent of the classical Greek concept of leisure expressed in the writings of Plato and Aristotle.

Worship is defined by Dahl as "that which is taking place when we consciously invoke the Spirit of God in some matter of private concern or in some corporate assembly" (1972, 8). Underhill defines worship as that "which leads the creature out from his inveterate self-occupation to the knowledge of God, and ultimately to that union with God which is the beatitude of the soul" (1937, 18). Through worship we reach into the spiritual realm and commune with God. We can worship God in songs and praising, in music and dance, but it is in silent prayer and meditation that we most clearly discern the nature of God and our place in God's universe. In prayer we are free to be ourselves, to cry unashamedly or rejoice loudly, to bare our uppermost hopes and our dominant fears. We are our most *authentic* selves in prayer.

Prayer and meditation, solitary reflection, and introspection all provide a means of finding one's true feelings and values, searching one's heart and soul, communicating with God and listening for God's messages, finding one's place in the universe, and achieving what Buhler calls "the integrity of the inner self" (1961, 371). Time spent reflecting upon life's meaning and purpose and our place in the scheme of life leads to a sense of personal integration and direction, self-understanding, and fulfillment. Quiet reflection and inward turning allow one to get in touch with personal feelings and to shut out the myriad distractions of the outside world.

The word "recreation" come from the Latin *recreare*, which means "to create anew." Recreation as contemplation and celebration of the divine through worship, prayer, meditation, and reflection provides a deep sense of refreshing renewal similar to that which follows a deep sleep. We are truly recreated and renewed and can experience the "peace that passes understanding" of which Jesus spoke. Leisure and recreation then are essentially spiritual. "A person discovers leisure when he

113

finds who he is, his uniqueness and worth as an individual, and his acceptance and relationship as part of the world around him" (Dahl 1972, 70).

Although our major thesis in this chapter is that leisure is essentially spiritual in nature, reaching its purest, highest form in the celebration and contemplation of divine worship, leisure may also include mental, physical, or social activities. The Greek ideal of "a healthy mind in a healthy body" long ago suggested the intimate connection of body and mind, the intertwining of physical and mental health. The more recent concept of holistic health is based on the interrelationship of body, mind, spirit, and emotion.

Walking, swimming, jogging, and other physical forms of exercise are a valuable form of leisure or recreation for people of all ages. The physiological benefits of exercise —improved cardio-vascular functioning, lowered metabolic rate, improved muscle and bone strength and flexibility—are well documented. Equally well documented are the psychological benefits derived from active participation in physical exercise—a natural "high," release of stress and tension through activity, better mental performance and alertness resulting from the increased flow of oxygen to the brain, improved body image, a healthy vigorous feeling, and increased poise and self-confidence. Exercise can take on a meditative quality. "The comingling of mind and body involvement massages the spirit, awakening a sense of the life-force flowing throughout all of nature" (Dangott and Kalish 1979, 71). As long as the activity is freely chosen, provides a sense of pleasure, and the individual is deeply involved in it, then the opportunity to achieve a true leisure state exists.

As a mental state or attitude, leisure allows for self-reflection, an inward turning, and the achievement of perspective. Erikson suggests that the major psychological task or crisis of late life is achieving a sense of integrity over despair. Integrity is possible only if one can come to view one's life as inevitable, meaningful, and worthy to have been lived. Similarly, Kelly proposes that through leisure the elderly can achieve a sense of personal integration, "a drawing together of various strands of the life course into a whole with meaning and coherence" (1982, 281). Robert Butler suggests that leisure in the form of contemplation and quiet reflection facilitates the life review, a natural, healthy process of remembering, analyzing, evaluating, and reconstructing the past events of one's life in order to achieve a sense of integration, meaning, and perspective, which helps one come to terms with one's own death and the death of loved ones.

Much leisure is focused on establishing or maintaining active involvements with family and friends or in the church or community. Such participation can help replace the void left by lost work and family roles, providing self-esteem, personal worth, and meaning formerly derived from work and family roles. Havighurst and Atchley suggest that leisure is a potential source of status and prestige, self-worth, and new friendships, as well as a way to be of service to others and relieve boredom. Kelly points out that leisure is a major context of social bonding and intimacy, because in leisure we are freest to be our most authentic selves.

The writings of the classical Greek philosophers and the teachings of Confucius and Zen, as well as the Old Testament and the teachings of Jesus stress the importance of learning and maturity through development and growth of knowledge, understanding, and wisdom. Modern-day philosophers and educators, influenced by these earlier thinkers, continue to proclaim the benefits of learning as a lifelong process.

When Jesus said (Matthew 18:3) "Unless you turn and become like little children, you will never enter the kingdom of heaven," he declared that childlike wonder and an openness to see new things are necessary for learning. Children possess a natural curiosity and receptiveness to learning. Goethe called this quality the "suspension of disbelief." Being able to pretend and use one's imagination are qualities that often disappear as one assumes adult roles and responsibilities. But "suspension of disbelief" is a prerequisite for creativity. Children enjoy learning. It is fun, a game of sorts. But too often our schools stifle this natural desire to learn. Learning becomes more of a chore than a game, and the joy and fun of learning disappear.

To mature and develop, to gain understanding and increase in wisdom, one must learn throughout life. To appreciate beauty in the arts, nature, and the world around us and thus to grow in wisdom, we need to retain some of the childlike wonder, natural curiosity, and the joy of learning. Jesus grew in stature and in wisdom.

The Scriptures are filled with references to knowledge, understanding, and wisdom. Wisdom is considered a precious possession; it is better than gold or silver or strength, and "makes one's face to shine" (Proverbs

16:16; Ecclesiastes 9:16; 8:1). In the Old Testament we read many accounts of major figures, such as Joshua (Deuteronomy 34:9) and Solomon (1 Kings 4:29), whom God filled with wisdom. We are commanded to act so that "we may get a heart of wisdom" (Psalm 90:12). Paul prayed for God to give the Ephesians the spirit of wisdom and knowledge (Ephesians 1:17).

In the Judeo-Christian view, old age is the summit of life and pinnacle of wisdom. Throughout the Old Testament we find references to the flowering of wisdom in old age and the veneration of older men. Similarly, Eastern philosophy, which encourages lifelong development of the inner self through introspection, creative processes, and spiritual processes, considers wisdom and spirituality the highest virtues of the aged. Among Tibetans old age is considered the best time for inner growth and contemplation. The ancient Greek seers also recognized the importance of maturity. They advocated that the proper time to study the most profound subjects, such as serious literature, the deepest philosophy, and the most complex science, was in later maturity, not in youth.

In these various sources we see an emphasis on human development, on progressive attainment of knowledge, understanding, and wisdom. Maturity is described as a lifelong process, not a particular state achieved at any one point in time. The path toward maturity is traveled over a lifetime and involves continuing change, inner growth, self-understanding, and spiritual development.

Aristotle, Socrates, and other Greek philosophers recognized the important connection between leisure, learning, and good living. Socrates proclaimed that "the aim of all education is to teach man to live the good life." The "good life" was a life of leisure, devoted to inner growth and development, mental creativity and expansion, and contemplation, the end of which was the achievement of wisdom and the virtues of honesty, freedom, justice, and truth.

Learning can be fun and enjoyed for its own sake. Lifelong learning is self-directed growth and development. Pursuing knowledge can meaningfully fill the abundant leisure hours of our later years. Learning for its own sake, pursued as an end in its own right, rather than as a means to some other end, is a joy and source of constant new experiences of self, God, and the world around us. Learning through nature, classroom experiences, or other means provides a constant source of mental stimulation and keeps one active and interested in life. It furnishes opportunity for creative expression and expansion throughout the life cycle.

The church can be a major force in helping older persons use leisure creatively. A 1975 study of religious participation by age group conducted for the National Council on Aging revealed that attendance was greatest among the old, and older individuals attached more importance to religion than those in any other age group. The elderly have been accurately referred to as the "new leisure class." A major mission of the church in modern society is to meet the needs of this segment of the population. The role of the church today, particularly with respect to improving life in the later years, is twofold: to educate members in the proper meaning and use of leisure and to encourage learning as a valuable, lifelong process. Today the church has the opportunity to help individuals achieve the more abundant life Jesus promised.

Many critics of the existing social system argue that our industrial, capitalistic society, which overemphasizes science, rationalism, materialism, and progress, has squeezed the beauty and joy out of our lives and made us slaves to money and machines. In *Work, Play, and Worship in a Leisure-Oriented Society,* Dahl suggests that in our society today our priorities are reversed. Currently we "worship our work, work at our play, and play at our worship," when instead we should "experience our work as play, see our play as worship, and make worship our work" (172, 116). Dahl argues that the church in today's society should be emphasizing the celebration of life as a gift of God and promoting the replacement of the Protestant work ethic with a new leisure aesthetic, in which we develop "new senstivity to the beauty and ugliness in life and to higher values of love, truth, justice, faith, and hope, man's place in the Universe, and his relationship to God and others." The church should also encourage experiences of transcendence in which we get in touch with "something deeper than our rational selves."

To suggest that one major role of today's church is to educate members in the proper meaning and use of leisure is not to imply the need for more entertainment, amusements, or frivolous forms of diversion. Nor is it a plea for more participation in physical activities and hobbies. It is, rather, to call for a return to the festive, joyous thanksgiving and celebration and the quiet, solemn reflection and serene contemplation that traditionally characterized Hebrew and early Christian

119

observance of the sabbath and holy days. To prepare individuals to celebrate the gift of life—to live in a zestful, festive, playful manner, appreciating and marveling at the beauties of nature and art, God, the Universe, one's self, and one's fellows—is to fully educate in the proper meaning and use of leisure.

Another major task of the church is to encourage learning as a valuable lifelong process. We should encourage individuals to take seriously the ancient maxim of Socrates to "know thyself" and seek self-knowledge and self-development. We should help people learn how to learn and come to love learning for its own sake. Increasing people's awareness of various nontraditional avenues to knowledge is essential. As Christ, Socrates, Thoreau, Emerson, and other notable figures teach us, we can learn from nature, the city, the arts, and people and things around us, as well as from books and classroom experiences. We who are in the business of providing spiritual leadership and promoting spiritual well-being should be more concerned that our society teach people "how to make a life," not just "how to make a living" (Mobley 1982).

In describing the important personal qualities that make an artist in aging, Gross et al (1978) listed the following: an intense love for life, the gift of enjoyment and the ability to give joy, a tendency to look at the positive side of life and find the good in people and events, a deep love and appreciation for beauty and nature, a love for people, modesty, optimism, and curiosity.

The church can help to make our last years of life our best and most fruitful.

Bibliographical information for this chapter can be found on page 194.

Creative Living Environments
for Older Persons
Charles W. Pruitt, Jr.

From the moment of birth, each of us is vitally affected
by the environment that surrounds and nurtures us. As
infants and throughout childhood we have limited control over the intimate setting in which we are sheltered
from the elements, fed, and first connected to the
outside world of schools and playgrounds. Our parents
or other adults guide the rhythms and choices of daily
living.

As we reach adolescence and move toward maturity,
we assume increasing control over our own homes and
families. This adult setting must reflect not only personal tastes and choices but the demands of work and
the needs of all those who form our primary relationships. This fact alone calls for a succession of changing
personal environments as we grow older and the compo-
sition of the family unit changes.

One can liken the changes selected or imposed over
the course of a lifetime to shifting stage sets. As children
we are placed in a scene created by our parents, and we
are expected to act out scripts that have, for the most
part, been written by them. As teenagers we participate
more and more in designing new sets and add new
themes and variations to the script. As adults we take

over the entire production. Within the limits of circumstances, we're free to move to a whole new stage. We can try new affects, improvise lines, fit the backdrops to the mood!

But in real life, unlike theatre, we act out our part only once. There are few rehearsals and no repeat performances. Each stage setting must be chosen with great care, because in every drama the scenery and the props are of crucial importance in successfully carrying out the developing story line. There are multiple, interweaving themes, each with its own requirements for authenticity.

So it is in the unfolding of our lives. For example, one theme of life is spiritual growth. Opportunities for spiritual development and nurture are a matter of great importance to most of us when we select a home. Proximity to a church of choice frequently becomes a key factor in the process of choosing a residence. And access to privacy within the home may have a direct bearing on the course of our inner journey.

But freedoms diminish as we grow older. We experience a gradual loss of control over many aspects of our lives. With the death of a spouse or diminishing personal health, we become increasingly dependent on our children or others to help us in selecting a stage that will allow us to maintain as much control as possible. This chapter is concerned with creating alternative environments for older adults that will have a positive impact on life-style, dignity, and safety, and provide maximum independence.

Most older adults resist changing their living situations unless it is a change of their choice. How often we hear an older person say, "I don't want to leave my home until I have to!" And *have to* usually means entering a nursing home or similar institution. All of us have a great fear of such an eventuality, as we know nursing homes to be negative living environments where we will lose most, if not all, of our independence. Many residents of these "homes" for the aging and infirm look upon them as jails. They refer to themselves as inmates, and not without reason.

We are all too familiar with the demographics of our aging society and the impact that life extension is having on our communities and institutions. The question and challenge before us is, What are we going to do about it?

American society is in an era of revolutionary advances in medicine, science, and technology. As in western European societies before us, our nation is experiencing a rapid increase in the numbers of older adults in its population base. Moreover, due to the continuing extension of the average life span, we are not dealing just with a larger number of persons sixty-five to eighty-five. Rather, we must now consider the needs and desires of many more persons over eighty-five and even over one hundred. This changing age-mix phenomenon poses completely new problems to individual older adults as they seek to enjoy their newfound longevity. Our society must assist in finding solutions to these problems and seriously address the issues arising around its aging population.

Philosophers have said that the manner in which a country deals with its older citizens is a true test of its morality. During the period 1980-84, I visited and studied elderly housing and long-term care facilities in England, Scotland, Denmark, Austria, Hungary, Russia,

China, and Hong Kong. It was fascinating to see first-hand the types of facilities and programs for older persons that have been developed in other countries. Each country's approach reflects its unique demographics, cultural patterns, and political structures. By and large, all of these countries have done well by their elderly, and most have adopted policies and programs aimed at providing a comfortable and purposeful old age.

The western European countries visited, the closest parallel to our own society, dealt with the demographics of aging and the similar aging issues we now face more than twenty years ago. Many of these countries have populations in which the over-sixty-five group exceeds 20 percent of the total. America will probably experience comparable percentages before the turn of the twenty-first century. In my opinion this bodes well for Americans, and I am confident that our society will respond in a similar manner in the coming years. We have the opportunity and necessity to develop new paradigms in which older adults can act out their extended lives in dignity and comfort. I am confident that churches, recognizing that a large portion of their members is over fifty years of age, will want to participate in development of such models.

In order to better understand and prepare for action, let's look a little more closely at how we got here, how churches have been involved, what the older person is like today, and some of the creative responses to the needs of this segment of our society.

From the beginnings of our country, churches of all denominations have provided shelter and care to the poor, the sick, and the old as an expression of concern and duty. Indeed, a key tenet of our Judeo-Christian heritage teaches us to honor our parents and elders.

In the eighteenth and nineteenth centuries, churches created poorhouses or almshouses where the suffering indigent were placed for care while dying. These institutions were the forerunners of today's nursing homes and homes for the aged. They probably were the root cause of the negative image such institutions have today.

With the dramatic advances in medical care and research in the early twentieth century, we began to see a radical change in these institutions. After World War I, facilities created exclusively for care of the old began to appear. Churches were the pioneers in sponsoring these homes, which often provided not only shelter but a variety of personal services. As their residents grew older, they added infirmary beds for those who could no longer function without round-the-clock nursing care. After World War II more church-related institutions were developed in response to the growing national attention to and concern for the elderly. And, for the first time, financial assistance came from the federal government.

The first White House Conference on Aging, held in 1961, brought into focus a national agenda of issues concerning America's elderly. Of prime importance at this trend-setting conference was the attention given to appropriate and adequate housing and long-term health care for the burgeoning older population. For the first time, the federal government was urged to embark on a major housing program specifically designed for the low- and moderate-income elderly. As a result, the Housing Act of 1964 created the Section 202 Independent Elderly Housing Program for nonprofit sponsors, under which over 200,000 affordable, specially designed housing units have been built, with occupancy restricted to low- and middle-income handicapped and persons over sixty-two.

Churches all over the country were sought out by the federal government to be sponsors of Section 202 housing, and they responded by the hundreds. In recent years church-related organizations have been active in sponsoring continuing care retirement communities that cater to the upper-income elderly. The primary attraction of these unique communities has been the assurance of nursing care when needed.

The mass media remind us constantly of the "problems" and "needs" of the stereotypical elderly. The census data, national polls, and university research studies tell us that *They,* the elderly, need and what a problem *They,* the elderly, are now and will increasingly become in the future. Clearly this ageist attitude is a symptom of a society in transition. The church and others who are developing residential programs for older persons must understand and come to terms with the strength and vigor of all the many exceptions to the aging stereotype. It is of the utmost importance always that we treat older persons as individuals and recognize the broad range of their personalities and circumstances.

I like to illustrate this point by suggesting that the functional capacity to perform the activities of daily living of a sixty-five-year-old in 1950 is generally comparable to that of an eighty-year-old today. Medical advances, improved nutrition and health habits, and higher incomes are the key factors in this remarkable advancement in average function by older persons. This phenomenon has been observed at homes for the aging by plotting the average age of new residents at the time of admission. The average has climbed steadily from 65-70 in the 1950s to 85-90 today, while the capacity to perform the activities of daily living has remained constant. If the trend continues, we may look for some remarkable ninety-five-year-olds by the year 2020!

It is important in our discussion to consider that growing old in our society is likely to occur over a thirty- to forty-year span. From this perspective, it is logical for individuals to anticipate an optimal requirement of several different environments during their old age.

Older adults are becoming better educated, healthier, and more vigorous. They will have more income and feel more secure in participating in community affairs. In fact, they will be "more everything," compared to today's elderly. Women will continue to comprise a large majority of older persons, particularly after eighty-five. But we can expect very different types of older women. They will be more independent, more financially secure, more likely to have had a career. Again, "more everything," compared to today's older women.

Those of us who work in long-term care of older persons must never forget that 95 percent of all older persons live independently in housing of their choice in the community at large. Only 5 percent ever live permanently in long-term care institutions or assisted living environments. We frequently make the assumption that all older persons are or will eventually be like this 5 percent. Fortunately this is not the case, and most Americans need not look forward to being confined to an institution.

All older persons prefer to live in an independent environment. If given a choice, they will invariably choose a community living environment that maximizes independence.

Institutions are usually age-segregated, that is, a minimum age requirement is a condition of residence. I have found that older persons are comfortable with age segregation in institutional settings due to the desire to associate with peers who like themselves cannot live independently in the community.

Taking this conclusion to its next logical step calls for the development of residential and long-term care facilities that will allow these changing types of older adults to realize new levels of potential for a full and productive longer life. The church can and should assist in developing models that encourage a high degree of self-worth and personal identity, settings that provide real opportunity for older persons to maintain good health, positive social interaction, a variety of recreation and creative activities, and continuing opportunities for spiritual growth.

Church sponsors should no longer be content to offer a single facility and expect it to provide everything an older person desires and needs over a thirty- to forty-year period. No longer appropriate for today's elderly, the typical church home for the aged must look for new ways to serve, both now and in the future.

In the past, the average church home has developed housing with nursing care as a response to the ever increasing health care dependency of its residents as they aged. Most homes converted residential spaces into infirmaries and nursing units. This was usually done a room or a floor at a time. The result is that these homes have lost the residential flavor created for the independent elderly, as they devote more and more space to the care of very frail and chronically ill residents.

Although almost all church homes were originally designed to serve the well elderly, they have succumbed to the notion that they should not relocate an older person when his or her medical needs cannot be met in a residential setting. Therefore, over a period of time, the typical home's program and structure has been modified to fit the physical health needs of the resident population. The inevitable result is that the well elderly for whom most church housing was designed find these homes are no longer acceptable.

What do we do to combat this situation? First, we must no longer cling to the belief that older people should not move from one facility to another when their health declines. The physical and emotional needs of an individual over a thirty-year period most likely cannot be met in just one type of residential or long-term care setting.

Government and private agencies are presently giving the highest priority to finding alternatives to institutionalization. Most gerontological planners agree on this worthy goal, but some of us find it difficult to reach a consensus as to what is meant by this generalization. My impression is that *institution* is being used to mean "nursing home." Now, as in the past, most nursing homes are perceived as being so negative that any other solution would be preferred. This is the result of traditional societal attitudes and public policies that remove the frail and sick elderly from the mainstream by placing them in nursing homes. Nursing homes are also a result of an irrational and splintered health care system that has focused on acute care and ignored the long-term care required by chronic conditions most likely to affect the elderly. Our contemporary health care system appears not to believe that old people's health can improve or that they may have potential for rehabilitiation. Rather, the health system's evident goal is simply to provide custodial care at the lowest possible cost. Needless to say, older persons resist nursing home placement mightily, and this attitude will not change until nursing homes change.

Are there viable alternatives? Can we create more housing for the elderly and long-term care facilities that offer positive living environments suitable for the new types of older adults emerging in our society? Here is a challenge for the churches to take up. Not only can churches sponsor model facilities, but they can call on the community's health leaders and government representatives to address and meet the needs of older persons.

Another role for churches is to monitor the performance and quality of care being provided by nearby personal care and nursing homes. A substandard nursing home near my home was closed recently due to the efforts of a dedicated group led by committed church women who were appalled by the conditions and practices there. Their courageous attack on the home and the regulating bureaucracy was remarkable. And they won.

Gerontologists and health planners generally agree that the ideal solution for older persons who have chosen to relocate from a completely independent living environment is to be able to choose from a variety of shelter options with access to long-term health care. Linking shelter and health care can provide a continuum of shelters and services over a long period of time. Americans have always had a strong feeling of community, and most elderly desire to stay where they are as long as possible. Their preferences, as well as their requirements, should be honored to the extent of our resources. However, *as long as possible* does not mean "forever," and at some point change becomes appropriate.

Again, it's important to remember that 95 percent of all older adults live independently in the community, much as they have all of their lives, and less than 5 percent are residents of nursing homes or other institutions. Clearly the overwhelming norm for older persons is to live in the community.

Figure 1 illustrates the range of environments that may be required by older persons. Shelter needs are seen to be static compared to the ever increasing social service and health requirements. Following the rising curves of need, the cost of social services and health care accelerates rapidly. Understanding the relationships of shelter, social services, and health care if critical to developing solutions.

Community Housing

We have noted that 95 percent of all older persons live in the community. However, the home settings vary

greatly. Older persons live in single-family homes, multifamily apartment buildings, rooms or apartments in
the homes of their children, hotel rooms, and mobile
homes. All of these styles are considered "normal" and
therefore are desirable to most older persons. But new
alternatives are gaining favor, and a wide range of proto-
types may already be found. What follows is a survey of
the variety of creative environments possible for the
aging.

Shared housing
One model rapidly growing in popularity is that of two,
three, or more older persons pooling resources to share a
house or apartment. The obvious benefits include
reduced housing costs, sharing of household chores and
cooking, and the companionship of others.

Many churches are considering how they can become
matching agents in the home-sharing process. Some
have established referral centers in their church to bring
together persons who are attracted to the idea. Others
cooperate with community-wide programs. In many
instances, the owner of a large home has decided to
invite others to move in on such a basis. Some early
home-sharing arrangements in Florida brought ten or
twelve persons together in one large home. Maids and
cooks were hired to handle routine household cleaning
and cooking.

Shared housing is not considered an institutional form
of elderly housing, as there is no third party involved in
the day-to-day management of the home. The sharing
partners initiate and benefit directly from the arrangement without outside assistance or control over their

daily lives. In the small town of Wellsboro, Pennsylvania, a doctor donated a large house across the street from his church with the understanding that the congregation would establish a family-style home for the elderly, with each resident paying his or her share of operating costs. A retired minister and his wife were appointed to guide this ministry. In Los Angeles, a nonprofit agency called Alternative Living for the Aging assists in forming similar small-group sharing arrangements for older persons. In a southern diocese, the Church Housing Commission has helped churches in several cities to convert parsonages into shared housing for groups of eight to ten men and women.

Since many communities possess an excellent stock of large homes, the shared housing concept will probably become more common and come to be an important resource to older persons who seek to reduce their housing costs, share in burdensome household chores, and find companionship among peers.

Multifamily housing
Older adults are increasingly attracted to multifamily apartment buildings and planned communities of single-family homes which provide new, smaller, and more compact housing units with centralized maintenance and security services. The chore and expense of maintaining large, older homes for just one or two persons is the primary motivation for selecting this option.

Such buildings and communities do not have age restrictions and are primarily marketed to young and middle-aged adults who also find this relatively carefree style of living very attractive. Most units only have one- and two-bedrooms so they do not attract families with children. Indeed, children are frequently not permitted.

It is likely more and more older adults will select this particular housing option in the future due to its convenience, relatively reasonable cost, and the security of nearby neighbors.

Housing for the elderly

Over the past twenty years there have been many multi-family apartment buildings specifically designed to house older residents, usually located in or near the center of stable neighborhoods. Although some planners and gerontologists discourage age-restricted housing, the older population has found these facilities much to their liking. Typically, buildings catering exclusively to the elderly have long waiting lists of applicants. Financed through private and governmental programs, independent elderly housing residents are characterized as active and healthy with an average age of seventy to seventy-five.

Churches have been heavily involved in initiating the development of such facilities. In many cases the church continues to be involved in the management and operation after the building is completed. Residents usually express positive attitudes toward such housing and remain until a health crisis precipitates the need for another location. The elderly housing buildings sponsored by the federal government have resisted the pressure to convert portions of the building to infirmaries or nursing beds. I believe that this position will insure the long-term success of this form of housing for the elderly.

Assisted Living

After age sixty-five many older persons suffer an emotional or physical incident that causes them to seek a supportive living environment in which others provide a personal service. Meals, bathing assistance, housecleaning, transportation, and dressing assistance are examples of personal services that allow individuals to overcome a lack of function in one or more areas. Spouses and children are the most common providers of these personal services; but if no one is available to offer assistance, the individual must seek other solutions.

Boarding home
Boarding homes are the simplest form of assisted living, offering one or more meals per day and a room. Usually they are large, older houses that can accommodate four to eight persons. However, they do not provide personal care services, and a resident who needs such help is asked to move.

Churches often find it feasible to offer minimum assistance, thus enabling people to remain in a relatively independent situation. For example, church members provide transportation for older persons attending worship each Sunday. Congregational support groups are organized to bring together young and middle-aged adults who are caring for an aged parent in their own home. Some churches provide regular luncheons or dinners for groups of older persons. Churches "adopt" boarding homes and organize friendly visitors to call regularly on residents and to provide telephone reassurance programs and special events such as outings and holiday meals.

Congregate elderly housing

A relatively recent mode of elderly housing with support services, congregate housing is most often a medium to large multifamily apartment building with a variety of common spaces, including a central dining room that provides one or more meals per day to all residents, lounges and recreation rooms, and spaces for health maintenance activities. A comprehensive array of personal services such as housekeeping, homemaker services, transportation, and temporary in-home personal care assistance are either provided by in-house staff or arranged for by management with community or public agencies. A minimum of one meal per day is usually required, whereas housekeeping and other personal services are generally optional, with charges based on units of service delivered. Congregate housing models developed since 1980 have been widely acclaimed as valuable resources in preventing or delaying nursing home admissions.

It is interesting to note that many of the earlier independent elderly housing buildings, now fifteen to twenty years old, have considered or are considering the development of congregate programs which provide a meal service and health maintenance functions. These program conversions reflect the additional services requested by long-term residents in order for them to remain in the facility. For church sponsors of existing independent elderly housing, the trend toward each conversion is an important consideration in planning for the future. All too often, sponsors cling to policies and definitions of service adopted years ago, which may be irrelevant to the desires and needs of the residents now being served.

Personal care home
Found in practically every community, personal care or group homes usually accommodate four to twenty-five persons in large family-style homes or former rooming houses. Frequently these facilities operate "submerged" from regulation or inspection by health and public welfare agencies, but most states have enacted, or are considering, legislation that establishes programs for licensing and regulation.

As most such homes serve primarily low-income persons, many states license and regulate them through public welfare departments that provide payments for personal care services. Licensed homes are required to have fire safety features and around-the-clock services such as dressing and bathing assistance, medication monitoring, planned diets, and general observation of the residents' daily activities. Well-managed personal care homes provide the frail elderly with a reasonably priced and comfortable living situation. As few of the homes employ registered or licensed practical nurses, most of the personal care services are provided by aides and attendants trained by the management. When on-site nursing services are required, the management arranges for public health nurses or visiting nurses to provide it on a regular or case-by-case basis.

Personal care homes, due to their small size and scattered locations, can be an excellent alternative housing resource for the frail elderly seeking a noninstitutional living arrangement. They will become increasingly important as alternatives to nursing homes because of their smaller size, more attractive accommodations, and the significantly lower cost per day.

Many individual churches are sponsoring personal care homes in their neighborhood or "adopting" a home located nearby. Through visitation programs and volunteer efforts, church members can improve the quality of personal care home operations. Regular visitation by volunteers is a powerful incentive to home managers to run a good facility.

Churches may be called upon to become active partners in sponsoring long-standing nonprofit personal care homes that at one time were church-related. Many communities have establishments of this sort that were begun in the early part of this century by church women's organizations.

Sponsorship in these cases involves taking on the responsibility for providing leadership for the operation and financial viability of the home and providing volunteers to relate the residents to the church and community at large.

Unfortunately, many of these homes have not kept up with the times. I recently met with the president of the board of one such home. A thirty-minute conversation made it evident that she had no idea what the home's role was in relation to other community facilities. She had no knowledge of how the home was licensed or why three administrators had resigned suddenly in the last two years. There were no current financial reports, and she could not recall if a budget had been adopted. At sixty-four, she was the youngest board member, and several members were over eighty-five. The home's admission policies and forms had been adopted in 1938 and had never been changed. A board committee, without staff present, interviewed applicants and decided who was to be admitted. Married couples, single men, and persons receiving public assistance were not eligible for admission. One board committee was responsible for the food service and supervised the cooks; another committee supervised housekeeping and the housekeeper; another, health care; and another finance. This home is only 50 percent occupied and no one is applying for admission. The board is frightened and puzzled, yet is considering expanding the unlicensed infirmary, as this portion of the home is full. The facility has a rich and important past, but its future is threatened, because of the inability of its board to understand and accept changes and respond appropriately. Its best hope is for the board to step aside and give the facility to a responsible organization, perhaps a church, that has the capacity to revive it and take it into the future.

Retirement community
The more affluent elderly have been attracted to age-restricted communities that offer both residential and nursing care services on a single site. The earliest of these full service communities were called "life-care communities" and offered a residential and health care service package for an actuarily computed entrance fee that guaranteed all care for life. Most such facilities, becoming known as continuing care communities, now

have a modified entrance fee, a life-use fee, and a monthly service fee.

Unfortunately, some of them have not achieved the occupancy levels and length of stays projected. The cost of nursing and other health care by residents has increased geometrically, because of inflation and the dramatic lengthening of the life expectancy. Put simply and callously, the residents did not die on time, resulting in severe operating deficits and bankruptcies.

Numerous variations on the life-care and continuing care theme are still being developed, based on some form of actuarially determined life-use projection. A national study of continuing care facilities conducted in 1982 by the University of Pennsylvania provides a wealth of data on these facilities. The study documents the need for regulation and inspection by states to ensure the protection of residents' payments and to ferret out unscrupulous developers who make their money and then abandon the project. Most states have adopted or are considering such legislation under insurance laws. Churches should consider carefully before developing a continuing care community financed under the life-care concept, because predicting the future is as problematic today as it was in the past. Further, this concept is susceptible to abuse by some for-profit developers and consultants/promoters.

There is little justification for churches becoming involved in this type of housing, because the high costs of development make it so restricted. Often church-related continuing care communities have been hailed as a great service to the community when in reality they serve a very small but affluent percentage of the elderly.

It seems to me that if churches wish to become involved in such developments, they should seek to insure that they will serve a broad segment of the elderly population in the community in which they are located. The church should give priority to developing housing for the low- and moderate-income elderly before considering facilities exclusively for the wealthy.

In the future, I hope church-related sponsors will develop multiple housing styles and long-term care facilities under one management that include many options from which older persons of all income levels can choose an appropriate environment. A few such operations with multiple housing styles are presently demonstrating that church-related sponsors can do this successfully. This mangement form may be the only feasible method of serving both the low- and moderate-income and the upper-income elderly in housing which offers a continuum of care in multiple settings.

Health Care

Long-term care facility
The terms long-term care facility and nursing home are used almost interchangeably today. Nevertheless, it is my fervent hope that nursing homes as we know them today may be replaced by a completely new form of long-term care environment.

The greatest fear of the elderly today is that of being forced into a nursing home. The negative image of nursing homes is not unearned. It is very difficult, almost impossible, to create a positive ambiance in the typically designed nursing home. Their design and operation are geared to the needs of the very ill and dying, not to the hopes of the living. True, there are a few exceptional nursing homes in our country today, but they are very few and, in most cases, very expensive.

A major issue in long-term care is the large number of patients in nursing homes that relies on public assistance or Medicaid to pay for their care. In most homes, the larger the percentage of Medicaid residents served, the less likely it is that the facility will be professionally staffed and managed. Increasingly, the inadequate reimbursement provided by state Medicaid agencies is forcing church-sponsored nursing homes to limit the number of Medicaid patient admissions. It puzzles me that the federal and state governments expect nursing homes to take care of Medicaid-supported residents at less than reasonable cost.

A number of new for-profit nursing homes refuse to admit Medicaid patients or require a contract for an additional payment to supplement the Medicaid payment, which is illegal. This trend could be a disaster for existing church-sponsored homes, because the new facilities will attract the church homes' private pay residents to their newer and more attractive facilities, while the church homes' private pay patients will be replaced by Medicaid patients. We should not expect either for-profit or nonprofit nursing homes to provide care at less than reasonable cost. Without question, the quality of care is going to suffer, and two separate levels of care will evolve. The result will be high-quality care for private patients and lower-quality care for Medicaid patients.

The majority of nursing home beds are run for profit, and investors are not likely to put money into nursing homes that are expected to provide a service at less than cost. Will for-profit homes choose to reduce the quality of care before they reduce their profit? Time will tell.

My vision of long-term care is not the typical nursing home of today. When one requires continuous skilled medical and nursing care, the surroundings in which these services are delivered do *not* need to be negative and depressing. Creative design and management can result in long-term care facilities in which one can still "live" and even "get better." To achieve these goals, facilities must be architecturally designed to foster progressive geriatric medical and nursing care in an attractive setting. Program and staffing must emphasize achieving the maximum potential for all residents. Through rehabilitation and restoration, many very frail patients can regain at least some degree of lost function and control.

Long-term health care facilities should offer three services. First, they should provide community outreach programs—such as outpatient services, adult day-care, respite care, in-home services, and preventive care—that will enable more older persons to at least defer admission. Second, they should provide high-quality geriatric nursing care. Third, they should offer medical programs that emphasize rehabilitation and restoration and aim at achieving maximum independent functioning for all patients.

True, some patients in long-term care facilities will have very limited potential for rehabilitation, but placing them in a vibrant, attractive setting will improve their circumstances appreciably. In the ideal facility, the program emphasis for the limited potential patient shifts from rehabilitation to recreation and creative activities that allow the best possible quality of life in terms of mental and emotional stimulus.

All sponsors, for-profit and nonprofit, should seek to improve the architectural and interior design of new and existing facilities in order to achieve the most attractive and residentially flavored environment possible. Privacy and comfort should be the byword of planners. Every patient should have a private sleeping space with a window and individual control over heat, air-conditioning, and lighting.

With innovations of this sort, the specter of "living out one's days in an institution" might be exorcised, at least in some small measure. Any alleviation of physical and psychic pain for these our brothers and sisters is service in God's name.

An increasingly important and growing health care program is hospice, for persons who are terminally ill. Hospice programs in the United States have generally been patterned after those developed in England.

The prevalent model is a coordinated community-based program that utilizes professionals and volunteers to provide medical care and social service counseling to individuals and their families. This holistic approach involves the development of a medical care and social service counseling plan that provides coordinated care in the home setting or in institutions when required. These programs frequently have affiliations with hospitals or nursing homes to provide inpatient care as a component of the overall plan. The primary service goal of community hospice programs is to help the clients and their families to accept the reality of death while making the clients as comfortable as possible. Emphasis is on allowing the client to remain in the home or normal family setting.

A second model is hospice programs organized and operated by institutions such as hospitals or nursing homes. They may set aside a wing or a specific number of hospice beds that are staffed by special teams who provide care and counseling to clients and their families, both in the institutions and at home.

Hospice programs can be of great benefit to terminally ill clients and their supporting family members or friends, who frequently must deal with extended periods of painful and emotionally draining terminal illnesses.

The frequent involvement of churches in the development of the hospice movement has been noteworthy and has insured that the spiritual needs of clients are considered along with their physical and psychological needs. As a reservoir of committed and caring volunteers, churches are an important resource for talent and skills to staff hospice programs and to help integrate them into the community at large.

Hospital

Older adults are by far the greatest users of hospital services, and as their numbers continue to increase, they will use an even larger percentage of total hospital days. As a result, the Medicare program, which partially pays for hospital care for persons over age sixty-five, has become the largest single source of revenue for hospitals, a fact which gives the federal government tremendous influence over hospital finances.

The recently adopted Medicare prospective payment program called Diagnostic Related Groups has radically changed hospital care for persons over sixty-five. Hospitals are now paid a predetermined amount for a particular diagnosis rather than the reasonable cost of the care provided to an individual patient. Under this system, if the hospital can provide treatment at a lower cost, a profit is earned. As the system encourages the earliest possible discharge of the patient, a greater emphasis is placed upon alternative services such as nursing home care and home health care.

The initial results of the DRG program has been a startling reduction in the average length of stay in hospitals by older patients. Another significant result is the earlier discharge of patients who require intensive skilled nursing care. This means patients discharged to nursing homes from hospitals are much sicker than in the past and more likely to require comprehensive post-acute nursing and rehabilitation services. Nursing homes are responding to this new type of skilled nursing patient by increasing staff and rehabilitation capabilities.

The federal government's success in reducing the average length of stay in hospitals has led it to initiate studies of applying a similar DRG system to the federal/state Medicaid program, the primary purchaser of inpatient skilled nursing care and intermediate care. The goal will be the same: to reduce federal and state expenditures for long-term inpatient nursing care. We can expect the next five years to be turbulent ones for both hospitals and nursing homes as they cope with the DRG program and other efforts by government to bring about basic changes in how long-term care is delivered and by whom.

As older people experience the inevitable changes that impact every aspect of their lives, churches will be called upon to assist them in a positive and supportive manner in meeting the challenge and opportunities of old age. Older persons should have the right to choose surroundings that allow them to retain maximum control over their life-style. Churches can play an important role in the creation of spaces that allow older persons to live their extended lives independently and with dignity.

No one can delay or avoid the inevitable physical and emotional consequences of old age. However, it is incumbent upon us all to make every effort to understand and support older persons as they struggle to retain their feelings of self-worth and some degree of control over their lives. Churches should do everything they can to organize congregational ministries on aging that support these personal goals.

In an ecumenical and positive church response to these challenges, a Roman Catholic church leased its vacant convent to a Presbyterian-sponsored organization at $1.00 per year for use as a personal care home for very-low-income older persons. Here we see a church with an asset joining hands with a church-related organization that had management and technical expertise. This cooperation stands as a model for other communities.

Churches can truly play a role in creating innovative modes of living for older persons. With imagination, thoughtful concern, and work, options can be made available in each community that will meet the broad spectrum of needs existing today. Our churches have a tradition of reaching out to help those in need. I am confident they will continue to do so.

FIGURE 1: Styles/Types of Living Environments Desired as One Ages

COMMUNITY HOUSING				ASSISTED LIVING			HEALTH CARE	
Individual Housing	Shared Housing	Multifamily Housing	Housing for the Elderly	Boarding Home	Congregate Elderly Housing	Personal Care Home	Retirement Community	Long-Term Care Facility	Hospital

Individual Housing	Shared Housing	Multifamily Housing	Housing for the Elderly	Boarding Home	Congregate Elderly Housing	Personal Care Home	Retirement Community	Long-Term Care Facility	Hospital
Single Family	Variable Sharing Arrangements	Apartment No Age Requirement	Apartment Minimum Age Requirement	Room Meals Linen Services	Apartment One or More Meals Optional Housekeeping & Supportive Services	Room Meals Personal Care Services	House Apartment Room Continuing Care One or More Meals Personal & Nursing Care Services	Outpatient Services Nursing Care Rehabilitation Services Hospice Care	Outpatient Services Acute Medical Care Rehabilitation Services

Health and Medical Needs

Social and Supportive Service Needs

Shelter Needs

60   100

Functional Age

Degree of Frailty

$ Costs Per Day

This chart was adapted by the author from Figure 1, "Housing Policy for Older Americans in the 1980s: An Overview," by Jerold S. Nachson and Morton H. Leeds, *Journal of Housing for the Elderly*, vol. 1, Spring/Summer 1983.

Death Preparation
as Life Enhancement

Eugene C. Bianchi

To be truthful from the start, we should admit that there
is no fully adequate way to prepare for one's own death.
At first blush, such an assertion would seem to deny the
purpose of this essay, but in fact it may be the only
honest way to begin. Moreover, it is a sound way to
launch reflection on preparing for death, because the
admission of our limitations points to the power and
depth of the phenomenon of death that hangs over each
one of us. We would like to be able to treat death like
any other important problem in life. Through science
and humanistic learning, we tell ourselves, the untidy
issue of dying can be worked into a schedule of priorities.
But such thinking is just part of the normal self-deception that seems to help us cope with life. We fancy
ourselves to be mature adults who know about death;
the media parade it before us daily, and we joke about
death and taxes as the only sure things. But this is not to
know real death and dying, because we are not personally involved. It is not our own death, the ultimate
lonely encounter with the cessation of our own existence,
with the final loss that summarizes all other losses for us
personally.

Although we cannot know death in a gripping way
(except for certain life-threatening events, e.g., illness,

accidents, war), we can take limited, valuable steps toward preparing ourselves for it. While we are unable to deal with our death under the actual circumstances of its occurrence, we can struggle against the unhealthy modern tendency to deny death through escape and avoidance. Yet the question remains for most people: Why dwell on such a morbid subject, one that raises some of our greatest fears? The answer is quite straightforward, though still difficult to accept. It is simply that growth and deepening of personhood depends on coming to grips with mortality in a concrete, individual way. Philosophers, theologians, and psychologists emphasize the paradox in the title of this chapter: that life can be enhanced through reflective meditation on death. In a mysterious way, what seems to be a denial of life becomes the hinge on which psychological and spiritual maturity turn. Major world religions underscore this point through a variety of symbols. For example, nearly all of Christianity's main symbols focus on the problem of death. The liturgical events of Christmas and Easter speak directly to our theme. Christmas brings hope for new life in the face of the darkness of death symbolized in the winter solstice. And Easter represents faith and hope in the victory of life over death. Such religious symbolism can be misused to hide the believer's need to struggle personally with the challenges of mortality, but Christian doctrines can also be interpreted more soundly as an invitation to enter the narrow path toward enlightenment/redemption through death.

We will divide our reflections into two sections: long-term thoughts in preparation for death and considerations when death is more proximate. This topic is all the more appropriate in our time, when nuclear megadeath hangs over us all, as the arms race continues to escalate perilously. Such social concern underlines another important theme running through these reflections. As we accomplish the conversions or personal breakthroughs at various stages of life by encountering death, we can be freed for fuller social responsibility. We become less driven by our own survival compulsions, more aware of our common plight with the rest of creation, and freed for ethical commitments for peace and justice. This social dimension of conversions through death-encounter is closely linked to creative aging. A great ideal of elderhood is the development of universal concerns and involvements; a mature elder has moved through neurotic fears of death to be able to embrace the major causes of humankind. These older people will be in the forefront of movements to preserve posterity from nuclear megadeath and curb other dangers to physical and moral life on the planet.

Long-term Preparation

We are so used to daily living that we miss the splendid mystery of being alive. Perhaps the greatest wonder of our experience of existence is to realize how tenuous and precarious a thing it is to be a living, feeling, thinking person. For this complex spark of life known as *homo sapiens* is surrounded by death or by the forces that lead to death. Heidegger has reminded us that the fundamental fact of existence is that we are creatures oriented toward death. This is not said to make us feel fearful, though that may happen when we grasp the fragility of

152

life over against the powers of death. Nor is Heidegger simply restating a biological truism that we know from the living/dying process of all organisms. Rather, he is calling us to regain a primordial human awareness of the compelling mystery of being alive in constant contention with death. We are only a few heart beats or a few breaths away from the end of our existence. The philosopher wants to awaken the poet in each of us to taste the wonder of it all. When we seize upon the fact that we are contingent, not absolute or necessary beings, we start to comprehend the drama of each person's existence, suspended for a very brief moment in cosmic history between the darkness that went before and the unknown death that lies ahead. In this scenario death becomes a mystery that is both tantalizing and terrifying; it attracts our deeper curiosities and at the same time frightens us with the threat of losses that seem final. The theologian Rudolf Otto spoke of God as a mystery that both entices and terrifies. These traits are found across cultures and across historical periods. The analogy between God and death is puzzling, but it points also to an interlinking of religous sensibility and the primordial experience of being alive toward death.

When should we prepare people to appreciate this life/death mystery? Since its truth begins not in old age but at birth, childhood is the place to start. Although the earlier stages of life are not the principal focus of this essay, a few reflections are in order. It is healthy that more people today are willing to help children learn about death, in keeping with their capacities at particular ages. This means an appropriate witnessing of dying and of death, as well as a growing confidence in being able to talk about death, especially when it closely affects children, as when a friend or relative dies. Adolescence is an especially important time to aid the young in understanding death. The teen years typically bring a turmoil of self-identity through sexual maturation and the uncertain prospects of entering an adult world. Youths in this stage are in an unusually good time to experience the mental and emotional pain of transition, of leaving behind the comforts of childhood and venturing into new terrain. Teenagers are often deeply affected by the death of a peer or by the loss of a parent.

The following period of young adulthood may be the least fertile stage for personal dialogue with death. For most people the decades of the twenties and thirties are a time of energetic striving to establish themselves in the realms of intimacy/family and work/career. In reasonably favorable circumstances, the youthful ego does not have a keen sense of its mortality. Life seems to stretch out with unlimited horizons; signs of decline are not apparent. Sensitive young people may show a genuine interest in learning about death and dying, but this is generally not an existential concern for themselves. It may be a blessing that young adulthood is absolved from proximate concerns about death, for during this phase of life, the young must develop independence and strength of character. Their talents must blossom in vigor for the sake of civilization and of the next generation.

Of course, these are only generalizations about phases in the life span; there will be many exceptions to the typical patterns. What counts in the process of death education is adapting theory and practice to authentic insights and feelings according to phases of life. Much can be done before mid-life to sensitize individuals about the challenges that will arrive in each of their lives. The seeds of psychological and spiritual growth can be planted; if young people are kept ignorant about the deeper issues, they may be unable in midlife to face the hard message of mortality. The failure of many men and women to negotiate in creative ways the physical, psychological, and social crises of middle age can be in part attributed to a lack of preparation in their younger years. For the many facets of the mid-life struggle are reducible in the end to coping with one's personal mortality. If one has not started to comprehend that this is the real reason for the malaise of the middle years, chances are that a person will accept the superficial nostrums for curing the doubts and perplexities of mid-life. People will try to escape the pain of growth through hyperactivity or withdrawal from action, through new romances, through buying bigger cars or boats, or by pursuing the myriad other distractions from the real issue.

Yet it is especially in mid-life that the most important long-term preparation for death can happen. In the period between forty and sixty, we encounter in a very personal way our death-proneness. We start to count the years from the end rather than from the beginning. Our bodies commence to bear the signs of aging, signs that marshal before us the limits of time, energy, and eventually, good health. Recognized or unrecognized, small "deaths" take place on various levels: Earlier dreams for a certain mode of family and intimacy may fade, or the youthful dreams of success in one's career may vanish. If we could learn to be quietly prayerful (that is, develop a habit of listening awareness) as these events assault us, we would know that we are being prepared for a new journey in the spirit. Embracing these trials reflectively and contemplatively, we come to understand that we are going through what Gandhi called "experiments in truth." We may need a spiritual guide or a psychological counselor or a supportive group to help us weather the difficult testing. But the training that stems from death-awareness can lead us toward greater personal wholeness and outward creativity.

Religion at its best, psychology in depth, and the philosophical search for meaning are wasted on the young. Of course, this is a badly exaggerated statement. Yet it is an attempt to focus dramatically on a kernel of truth, namely, that the religious-psychological-philosophical seeker can embrace the hard experience of paradox, mystery, and depth only when he or she is ready for it. Given our lust for life and our unconscious fear of death, it is unlikely that we will be ready for the new journey before middle age, when, like it or not, the footsteps of O'Neill's iceman sound more distinct to us. Admittedly, there is a certain fear, perhaps even terror, involved in allowing intimations of our own death into our minds and hearts. The contrast in mid-life is particularly shocking; we may be at the apex of energies and accomplishments, while the signs of old age and death declare themselves in graying hair and wrinkles. These experiences can be great turning points in life. Will we make the transitions of mind and soul away from the narrower dreams of youth and toward lives of fuller introspection, empathy, and compassionate commitment to wider concerns of humanity?

Introspection, contemplation, or inwardness are relatively foreign notions in our culture. Yet they are indispensable in finding one's truer self in mid-life. There can be no death preparation as life enhancement without some cultivation of an inward life. This does not mean giving up active pursuits in one's career and social life. Rather, it involves dedicating some time, preferably each day, to helpful forms of solitary contemplation. Many simple techniques for quieting and centering are available in books, as well as in course offering and private instruction. Even as little as ten or fifteen minutes a day of silence and solitude can fulfill this purpose; but one must be motivated to make that time as sacred and intentional as the most important of life's activities. This gradual, personal journey beyond our fearfully controlling ego-consciousness allows us to break through the facades that hide us from ourselves, that is, from the deeper reaches of our our souls.

Some of these periods of prayerful listening to inner voices may be dry, tedious, and distressing. This may be especially true in mid-life, when thoughts of losses, failures, paths not taken, and the curtailing of time press in on us. These kinds of seemingly negative experiences, joined to the occasional dryness or apparent sterility of contemplative periods, are the narrow passages that may lead us to the edge of doubt and ambivalence about life. Yet these dark nights of the soul, as the mystics referred to them, are the points of encounter with death in life. In Jungian language, this can be represented as the ego learning hard but necessary lessons from its deeper self; in classical lore it is portrayed in the figure of Hermes, the youthful, active messenger, sitting at the feet of Hades to learn the secrets of the underworld. The encounter with one's finitude in the middle years, whether expressed in psychological or religious idiom, is an event at once illuminating and painful. One becomes more familiar with the neglected opposites within one's own personality: shadow aspects, repressed child, devouring mother, rejected feminine or masculine sides. From a religious standpoint, the suffering facets of these encounters can be ways of symbolically meeting the crucified deity within, the God who is a suffering fellow traveler in our inmost soul. In all of this, we are dealing directly with death as woven into the very fabric of existence. Sometimes these moments of solitude and contemplation will be filled by a void of calming peace; at such moments the broken strands of our life, our old wounds, find a healing balm.

Meditation on death puts us in touch with our finitude; in the middle years an experience of finitude can be the catalyst for developing one's own religiousness or spirituality. This is not a flight in desperation to a religious solution out of personal fears. Rather, an encounter with our own finitude, by making us more conscious of intellectual, physical, and moral limitations, tends to relativize the hold of institutions over us. The "oughts" of church, family, occupation, and the state are less constraining. We understand, perhaps for the first time, that in the end we must take responsibility for our own decisions and actions. Developing one's own spirituality needs the insights of tradition and a renewed grasp of the values mirrored in history. But these insights and values are appropriated in ways congruent with personal conscience; they are not merely rules imposed from without. Although it might seem that cultivating one's own spirituality is an eminently individual process, the surprising truth is that important social consequences flow from the contemplation of finitude. By freeing us from a rigid, external code of conduct, such contemplation enables us to criticize institutions and regulations as we work toward humanizing them and adapting them to current needs. Moreover, by being less bound to conventions of thought and action, we are opened to new levels of creativity. Instead of using energy to defend ourselves against threatening ideas or challenging persons, we can allow novel events to enter into conversation with a self-directed personality that knows the limits of all things.

At the heart of this development of one's own spirituality through reflection on one's finitude is a deeper experience of faith. Faith is frequently misunderstood as a collection of beliefs connected with certain moral practices and rituals. Yet faith must be distinguished from these religious manifestations. Faith is an attitude and act of profound trust in the face of death with its ultimate threat of annihilating all meaning. Faith is an action of releasing the walled-off self into communion with a benvolent and sustaining Reality that pervades a death-oriented cosmos. In its depths, it is a kind of letting-go that only that person can perform who understands from his or her own life the final transitoriness of all things. At this level, beliefs and practices assume a new position in our outlook; they may be carriers of meaning and grace inasmuch as they are suffused by faith. The faith that flows from meditation on death also liberates the imagination to craft and embrace a fuller unity in pluralism that transcends the narrow barriers of nation, race, and creed. Finally, such faith keeps us from falling into the paralysis and disintegration that afflict many who are not able to cope with the indications of their own aging and death. A kind of psychological death occurs when an individual tries to deny the signs of finitude in neurotic modes of withdrawal from life or of heedless plunging into youthful activities. Such a person is clinging fearfully to life as a possession to be defended against death, rather than as a gift to be shared to the end. Faith gives one the courage to break through those temptations and infuse life with hope and meaning in ever richer ways as death approaches.

Long-term education in light of death might seem to be a very private affair. This essay has stressed the personal dimension of this introspection, but the social aspects of such reflection have great significance. Among modern thinkers, Ernest Becker makes one of the strongest cases for the link between fear of death and social evils. He depicts a powerful unconscious motivation to repress the terrors of death by defending ourselves and our immediate group at any cost to others. Humans all too eagerly transfer their independence and self-initiative to leaders who promise to protect them against dangers to life. This concentration of power in hierarchies causes leaders to abuse outsiders who threaten the tribe and to oppress their own people. At the root of Becker's explanation of personal and social evil is the all-pervasive fear of one's own death, coupled with a relentless desire for immortality. Fearful anxiety before the world's overwhelming perils calls for the spilling of blood and other hurtful actions to expiate guilt and gain immortal life. Cruelty to outsiders becomes a kind of torture rite that convinces the perpetrators of their own life power, while denying it to others. We do in our fellow humans out of the fear of losing our own lives.

Although Becker's views merit critical comment and much nuancing, they dramatize an all too pervasive tendency in individuals and groups to preserve ourselves at terrible costs to others. Yet we need to know the worst in us to realize possibilities for the best. Along the introspective journey of meeting the terror of death, we can be transformed into persons who see and act in ways directly opposed to destructiveness. Through this kind of gradual education, death can become an ambiguous guest in our souls, inspiring both fear and hope. While we will always be anxious about our own death, we can come to understand the common bonds of our creaturehood, our fellowship with death-prone humanity and nature. When this experience is graced by the faith described above, potentials for empathy and compassion arise. We experience ourselves as companions with others in survival rather than competitors for a chimerical immortality. Thus an ethical orientation arising out of a continuing dialogue with death as both fearful and wisdom-bearing could lead to a new spirit of empathy, of sharing and of co-humanity.

This new ethical spirit, born out of personal conversion through encounter with finitude, manifests itself in mid-life as we begin to see our professional and other commitments in a new light. Work becomes more than simply a means for escaping deeper questionings, or for immortalizing ourselves through dominance over persons and nature. Rather, our work evolves towards being a flexible means for spiritual exploration and for service of a wider community. The ideal is that of a contemplative in action, a person fully involved in the world, yet not seeking to possess it for purely personal ends. This implies a spiritual transformation of work that allows us to appreciate and enjoy wordly matters for their own sake, while we seek to surround them with the structures of truth and justice. Our life becomes ever more outwardly focused in service and in being mentors to others, while at the same time our inner life is enriched.

This is not some airy and unattainable ideal. Dag Hammarskjöld, an early Secretary General of the United Nations, left a rich spiritual journal, *Markings,* that depicts his inward transformations while his days were outwardly consumed in serving as an international statesman. Hammarskjöld, who died in a plane crash while negotiating a dispute in Africa, also witnesses in his journal to a growing understanding of the meaning of his life in terms of his own finitude. Dorothy Day, pacifist and servant of the urban dispossessed, through her writings and her activities in the Catholic Worker Movement also left a testament of profound contemplation in action. Her memoirs, *The Long Loneliness,* reveal the transitions of a soul increasingly dedicated to charitable actions and at the same time deepening her own inner life in a spirit of radical contingency.

Intrinsic to developing the social compassion and commitment noted above is a change of attitude toward power. The exercise of mental, emotional, and physical power or energy is part of what it means to be human.

Youth stresses the exercise of power as mastery or dominance to protect and enhance the ego. Problems arise when this mode of power becomes the sole way of relating to the world for the whole life span. Technological society accentuates dominant power through the manipulation and control of external reality. Fear of death, the greatest loss of power, all too frequently leads to injustices and other forms of destructiveness. The social evils deriving from hatred, malice, and selfishness are connected with our understanding of power as dominance.

The shift from dominant power to serving or enabling power is closely linked to a creative dialogue with death and finitude in mid-life. In this dialogue we realize how futile and destructive has been our embracing of dominant power to preserve ourselves against various forms of death. As we find the faith to let go of self-preservation, we also discover forgiveness for our immersion in the violence of dominant power over others. We move gradually to cultivate a kind of eliciting or enabling power that allows others to respond authentically and humanely. This nonviolent power represents a significant change in our attitude toward the world. We no longer seek to use self-serving force, but in the charity that seeks union with what is loved, we allow others genuinely to exercise their own energies. Perhaps this is one of the greatest experiences to which persons in mid-life are invited: to substitute, for the power that promises to preserve the ego against adversity and death, a new power that, by releasing us from the all-consuming lust for self-survival, allows us joyful love of our deepest self and of others.

Meditation on personal death can also become an occasion for deepening our friendships and intimacies. When we become conscious of unhealthy defenses against death, in faith we can release some of our fearfulness. As we do this, our attitude towards family and friends can change; we can permit more of our true selves, with our illusions and vulnerabilities, to appear. Since we realize that time is not on our side, we can risk mutual revelation, trusting that the other can support the truth about ourselves. We long to reach beyond appearances, to touch and be touched by others at the center of our being. Knowing our common mortality can expand our sense of compassion and care. The middle-aged, for example, can reach out across generations to respect and stimulate the potential of younger people, and to relate with care to the older generation. In this process of enriching our friendships as we encounter our own finitude, there is a paradoxical joining of pain and joyfulness. It is painful to become more accepting of our weaknesses, hostilities, and self-deceptions; yet, when we have been educated in the school of death, we can also regard more lightly matters that we might otherwise take too seriously. In a seemingly contradictory way, an ability to invest one's work with a certain zest, lightness, and humor depends on a personal acceptance of death. We know in a new way that our activities will not ultimately preserve us; work, then, divested of false expectations can become a form of play, especially if it is conducive to one's personal growth.

What we have said about middle age concerning preparation for death as life-enhancing can continue to be the basis for a creative elderhood. But the last phase of life, from about sixty onward, has its own particular qualities. Death itself becomes a more proximate reality than it was previously. New limits and diminishments may gradually depress persons, especially if they have known good health throughout life. Losses of friends and intimates further impact on elders. Many suffer a loss of role significance through retirement; others with limited economic means worry about basic health care and adequate living conditions for themselves and their families. Moreover, these new problems of older age must be faced in an ageist society, which advances negative stereotypes about being old. The elderly may themselves embrace these debasing attitudes, thus bringing about a premature sort of psychic dying that opposes dealing with death constructively. Any combination of these considerable challenges can pull an elderly person downward into depression, hopelessness, self-deceit, flight into the past, loneliness, and a general withdrawal from vital living.

These are some of the real dangers of elderhood, and they are exemplified all too often in the contemporary world. Precisely because these issues have such dire consequences in old age, the personal transitions of attitude and spirit from mid-life on take on paramount importance. If transformation of values progresses from middle age, there is a good chance for what Teilhard de Chardin called growth through diminishments. Refined in the crucible of their own sufferings and sacrifices, such elders are gradually purified of egotism but develop fuller self-esteem. Their trials teach them greater truthfulness that lessens self-deception and makes them wise guides for others. They seem able to infuse their lives with quality time, even when the quantity of sand is smaller in the top of the hour glass. Instead of the inflexibility sometimes associated with the old, these elders go through a self-reidentification process. This means fulfilling some of the unmet needs and desires that went unrealized in earlier years. To summarize these gracious developments in such older people, we can say that in the very face of death they experience a greater freedom from the fear of death.

What needs to be stressed, however, for these spiritually advanced elderly persons is their calling toward universal concerns. The tendency of our culture is to confine the elderly to private pursuits at the periphery of societal life. As the older person is pushed out of the centers of action and decision making, outstanding skills, talents, and insights are lost to the community. The vocation of older people is to go beyond advocating merely the interests of their elderly peers to take on a spirit of stewardship for all life. With less to lose and fewer egotistical compulsions, these humanely advanced older people can achieve the apex of their careers as reconcilers. Reconciliation of destructive alienations at all levels of existence is perhaps the greatest New Testament ideal, seen in the Sermon on the Mount and in the letters of Paul (Gal. 3 and Eph. 2).

This reconciling work can take many forms, such as educational efforts toward needy young people or special services toward the elderly, especially those who are frail, confined, and poor. The elderly must also take up positions of leadership and consultation in secular and religious organizations. This does not mean that it is wrong for the old to enjoy privacy, leisure, and other pleasures. Rather, it is a matter of emphasis and responsibility. The elderly have a wonderful contribution to make to the great needs of the world through their knowledge and expertise in many fields. Moreover, the elderly have a special calling to work as reconcilers concerning the great issues facing humanity: questions of war and peace, justice and human rights, nuclear dangers, and population/ecological matters. This task of reconciliation and peacemaking can also be accomplished in quiet, personal ways through direct contacts with other individuals and through the courage and kindness that many older people show in sickness and hardship.

In these ways, the downward physical slope of life can become an upward spiritual ascent for self and others. Such peacemaking elders have a real future for themselves in the quality of their last phase, in their contributions to those who will succeed them; and for the faithful, many also find a future in hope for a life with God after earthly death. Most elders will need support systems—formal and informal, age-integrated and age-homogeneous—to help them realize these noble goals. When we speak of the old embracing universal concerns and returning to the centers of decision making, we are referring mainly to those increasing populations who enjoy reasonably good health into their later years. Yet there are also many with physical limitations who continue in elderhood the works of reconciliation; these are the persons who have successfully negotiated the psychospiritual transitions of mid-life and the period sometimes called that of the "young old." This creative aging differs in important ways from visions of longevity propagated in current literature on life-extension. The latter stresses quantitative dimensions of living longer; yet what finally matters is the quality of life in the last season. It is ultimately a matter of beauty, of building a mosaic with one's life. In Heidegger's idiom, this means learning gradually to dwell poetically in the world. Since great poets have always been able to express the human dilemma with finer clarity than the rest of us, we can sum up these perspectives in the words of William B. Yeats:

> An aged man is but a paltry thing
> A tattered coat upon a stick, unless
> Soul clap its hands and sing, and louder sing
> For every tatter in its mortal dress. . . .
>
> *Sailing to Byzantium*

Proximate Preparation for Death

When the Scriptures tell us that we know not the day nor the hour, they remind us about a sober truth concerning death. Though we are certain that we will die, the actual event will always remain something of a surprise. This is an important note to keep before us as we address proximate preparation for death. For most of us there will probably be a gradual passage from long-term to proximate encounter with our own dying. We may sense a substantial weakening of organic functions; chronic illnesses may hold stronger sway; we will probably have intimations that the end is not far off. This dying trajectory will be shorter for some when accidents, strokes, or heart attacks intervene. In addition to pain, fatigue, and other hardships, the approach of death will make us more dependent on others. In a culture that prizes independence and self-determination, new dependency will induce feelings of being a burden, of being valueless. The dying process, therefore, will deeply test one's sense of self-worth and self-respect.

An important preparation for these final phases of life consists in putting one's house in order in very practical affairs. This may mean writing or updating a will. It can also involve such concrete aspects as making sure that survivors know where to find documents, keys, and accounts. How do we want to dispose of our bodies: through burial, cremation, or donation to medical or scientific study? Many shy away from dealing with such issues, sometimes out of negligence, but probably as often out of fear of facing their own deaths. Yet these pragmatic matters are significant occasions for gaining perspective on optimal ways to use remaining time; moreover, these mundane concerns provide the context for showing love and care for others. Focusing on such questions may also have the salutary effect of reminding us to finish personal business, that is, bring to closure uncompleted relationships inasmuch as we can. We may need to receive or grant forgiveness, to heal wounds still festering in our souls, or to tell others that we love and appreciate them. Various forms of life-review have been developed to aid individuals with a counselor or in groups to search personal history for points of trauma, transition, and overall meaning.

In our age of heightened medical technology, we must think ahead about extraordinary measures to sustain our existence. The controversies concerning living wills and methods of euthanasia have raised ethical questions in many circles. But ultimately we must decide for ourselves, while we are still in a position to reflect consciously on the question. Living wills are not legally enforceable in most states, but a clear statement to kin or doctors may well influence how life-preserving technology is used. Husbands and wives, elderly parents and their children, and all others who will exercise special responsibility in such decision making should explore moral and humanistic aspects of dying with dignity. The quality of life becomes a crucial factor in determining whether it should continue. While direct euthanasia is fraught with potential for abuse, the pain and disability of individuals (some long before the imminent coming of physical death) may so lessen the meaning of life for them that a merciful death is preferable. Dialogue on these issues may curtail guilt, remorse, and depression for those survivors who were involved in the decision to terminate life-sustaining mechanisms.

It is difficult to know beforehand how we will react when we learn that our situation is terminal. "Terminal" may mean months or perhaps a longer period; it may be signaled by a newly-discovered disease or by a gradual breakdown through chronic ailments. Of course, we understand that we are all in a terminal state, but when it becomes proximate and relatively certain, intense psychological reactions often occur. It may be helpful, therefore, in preparing to meet death in a way that fosters gracious final living, to rehearse some typical responses to the announcement that death is imminent. Moreover, the emotional reactions and defense mechanisms need to be personalized as much as possible: How do *I* generally respond to bad news, to traumatic events? A common early reaction is fear and depression or sadness; that which is most precious to us, life, is about to be lost. We fear the deterioration, pain, and incapacity that may accompany the last part of our journey. We commence grieving over the loss of family, friends, and future.

Imaginative meditation can partially summon up these feelings. In quiet contemplation on our own last trajectory, we can acknowledge painful emotions, giving them a rightful place without denial or distraction. By permitting these feelings to come alive concretely (in reference to particular persons, our own body, etc.) in meditation, we can eventually arrive at an attitude of letting go. This letting go is a form of acceptance that brings a measure of inner peace. It is not a passive resignation to the destructive course of an illness. Rather, by working through some of these difficult emotions, we may be better able to marshal healing energies to resist the disease. A kind of emptying out of excessive fears is a necessary precondition for the type of meditative healing methods fostered by the Simontons in the book *Getting Well Again.*

Still other emotions challenge one whose death is proximate. Anger, whether expressed covertly or openly, will frequently arise. A primitive but useful function of anger is the mobilization of physical and mental energies to defend against attack. Whether we rage against God, humans, or natural forces, the true meaning of this anger is a gathering of energy to cope

171

with the deadly reality, to maintain a sense of self-meaning and integrity to the end. The anger may be more intense if the afflicted person is younger; a sense of injustice may prevail about a life cut off before its full flowering. Anger may fluctuate with depression and feelings of guilt; we may be guilty about being angry at relatives and attendants.

Some experience guilt for seeming to cause their own illness, or because they see the condition as a punishment from God. They may also feel guilty for having to abandon their responsibilities toward family and friends. Feelings of shame further aggravate the emotional response to one's own dying. We may be ashamed of our physical condition; we know that others do not like to associate with persons who look bad, who may be incontinent, tired, and depressed. Shame can stalk the dying who worry about their unusual behavior and their increasing dependence. Can we in meditative imagination pass before ourselves anger, guilt, and shame, as these reactions would be demonstrated in our own way? Can we think of concrete instances in which we have experienced these feelings and then transpose these reactions in imagination to our dying process? Such contemplative working-through over a period of time may prevent an excessive acting out of these emotions in the actual situation of dying.

Dealing with one's own death as a proximate happening is one of the most powerful challenges we will ever face. In light of this threat to the psyche, we must learn to respect the coping mechanisms in ourselves and others, as we try to adjust to the imminent reality of death. Various forms of denial, for example, have a positive purpose in that they allow an individual to rally energies for the confrontation. Denial, whether direct or indirect, can be an appeal for time to muster one's forces for grappling with the final mystery of life. Some may even carry on a pretense of denial to the very threshold of death, although they know interiorly that they are moribund. This is not an ideal way to die, but it may be a mode of courage for those who do not want to upset loved ones. On the other hand, there are clearly negative dimensions to denial. It can keep a person from completing unfinished business on material and human levels; it may very well hinder the individual's ability to heighten the quality of life before death. One's way of communicating with terminal people should be such as to permit the dying person to initiate discussion of the situation. Being present to the dying in a natural and caring style may elicit the deeper conversation, while respecting the boundaries of that person's integrity.

We dwell on these psychological reactions in the dying process to deepen our empathy. It is not enough to know the clinical patterns concerning death nor to amass data about the best places for the dying time. While there are important differences regarding home, hospital, or hospice care for terminal people, the overriding issue for our benefit and that of the dying is to learn empathy for the life phase that most of us will experience. Such understanding is very difficult to attain, because we find it hard to reflect with realism and sympathy on this frightening phase of existence. Yet if we learn empathy through meditation on death and through visiting or working with frail or terminal persons, we will be better able to sustain their dignity in the last season. As our fear of the dying process diminishes, we become sources of security and even hope for the dying. Helping others to die with dignity and hope can be enhanced by a spirit of faith. The latter may take the more traditional forms of religious language, or it may be expressed in less familiar idiom. The last hours of Aldous Huxley's life, for example, are movingly described in his wife's memoirs, *This Timeless Moment*. Laura Huxley performs a kind of verbal liturgy at her husband's deathbed. She encourages him, as he had done for others, to let himself go, to release himself toward the light.

The Huxley reference is just one example of the many rituals of death that can have rich meaning for terminal persons while they are still alive and also for their survivors. Surely we can all cite certain funeral rites that have been inappropriate, superficial, or hypocritical. But the need persists to surround the great moments of life with a special time and place, with dramatic memorials that make sacred these major passages. These communal celebrations, when done with sensitivity and respect, aid the survivors to accept losses, to be upheld in grief and mourning, and eventually to be welcomed back into full engagement in life. We are beings who create meaning through symbol and story. Although the dying time is often filled with weakness, distress, and possibly pain, it can also become the hour of final reenactments in which we strive to gather into a healing wholeness the disparate strands of life. These rituals, whether formal or informal, can be touchstones of our finest humanity. A dying young nurse was calling for the simplest of these rituals when she said to the hospital attendants:

I know, you feel insecure, don't know what to say, don't know what to do. But please believe me, if you care, you can't go wrong. . . . Don't run away. . . . All I want to know is that there will be someone to hold my hand when I need it. I am afraid. Death may be routine to you, but it is new to me. . . . If only we could be honest, both admit of our fears, touch one another. If you really care, would you lose so much of your valuable professionalism if you even cried with me? Just person to person? Then, it might not be so hard to die. . . .

Conclusion

Reflection on death, especially on one's own death, in long-term or in proximate scenarios, can enrich the aging process. Contemplation of personal death can spur one on to make the most of the present, whatever one's age. Such contemplation is not an exercise in morbidity for those who have started to work through the transitional crises of mid-life. My death, while always fear-inspiring in some ways, can also be seen as part of the natural cycle of all living creatures. Christians can learn a corrective lesson from naturalists on this point.

Christianity has so stressed the tragic dimension of death as a consequence of sin that it often loses sight of the natural aspect of dying as part of planetary rhythm and obscures an equally valid biblical perspective. For the doctrine of creation focuses on the goodness of the natural order, including its cycles of birth and death. Although the evil results that flow from sinful proclivities can bring about tragic and premature physical death

175

(e.g., crimes, wars, ecological destruction), the main connection between sin and death is on the level of the human spirit. The truly dire consequence of sinfulness is death of the spirit, the dehumanizing of individuals and groups, not the death of the body as a natural event. Our physical life today results from billions of years of cosmic evolution, marked by constant patterns of birthing and perishing, of spring and winter. The linking of death with sin is a very recent phenomenon, in evolutionary terms; the death that has any meaning in this context is the demise of human potential to know and love in the most human way.

A comprehensive view of death for persons of faith places it within the natural, God-established order of the universe. Acceptance of this mode of coming to be and of passing on becomes an act of fidelity to God's providence. Such reflection helps us develop a mystic sense of belonging to a greater whole, of being part of a trustworthy purpose in the world as we make our particular contribution to what Whitehead called the creative advance. On one level, this style of meditating on death puts us in touch with Lovejoy's vision of the chain of being: Our living and dying is joined with the life and death of all other creatures in that we mutually influence one another. In this view, our deaths serve to fertilize the garden of earth. On another plane, we can enter early into our dying by way of personal trust. This approach is expressed graphically in a memorable story told by Lawrence Jones about an experience with his son: The mode of trust in God concerning our death is

176

represented through an analogical experience of child-parent trust:

Down at Fisk University we had a stone wall that ran the length of the campus. My son used to like to get up on that and run. Sometimes he would run along in the evening near huge oak trees that hung over Eighteenth Avenue. There was a light in between, so that there was light and shadow. He would get up on the fence and run along in the light. Then when he got to the darkness he would jump down and take my hand. We would walk through the darkness together until we got to the light again. Then he would jump on the wall again and run. That began for me to be analogy to our relationship with God. My son knew the father that he saw in the light and whose hand he held in the dark would not change because the circumstances had changed.[1]

Whether described in traditional religious idiom or in other ways, a personal, meditative encounter with our own dying can enhance life as a time of adventure and celebration. When our living is enfolded within the mantle of the acceptance of death, each day has the potential for being a new venture. Every night we can prayerfully seek to free our minds from crushing or paralyzing events of the past, so that each morning begins a day of novel opportunities, of new beginnings. This is not a pollyanna escape from our history; the latter should always be present to us with its lessons for life. The point is rather that as we open ourselves to a listening dialogue with death, the wounds and failures of the past impede us less from venturing hopefully into each new day.

In this sense, even our dying day can be approached as a new happening, an adventure. If life has been a series of adventures for a person, death may be looked upon as a door to still other revealing experiences. This attitude arises from a spirit of faith and hope in the benevolent energy and presence of God. Such a spirit is not necessarily a flight from facing death in the hard reality of its suffering and diminishments; nor is it a childish demand that God reward us with life everlasting because we have been good on earth. Rather, it is a serene conviction that the best of us passes on into a new adventure within the One who is greater and more beautiful than we, to paraphrase a statement of Teilhard de Chardin.

It may seem strange to speak of death as a final celebration of life. Yet that is precisely the paradox of faith. Perhaps the greatest grace we will ever experience is that of celebrating what has been and what is, as we draw near to our death. This is a special gracing for which our whole life can be a preparation. To celebrate is to rejoice for having experienced life with its pains and joys, to be glad that we have helped our survivors to preserve and nourish the beautiful, fragile gift of life into yet another season. In his spiritual memoirs Dag Hammarskjöld summed up perfectly this embracing of the world in celebration at death: "Night is drawing nigh; for all that has been, thanks; for all that shall be, yes."[2]

Notes

1. Eugene Bianchi, *Aging as a Spiritual Journey* (New York: Crossroad, 1982), p. 250.
2. Dag Hammarskjöld, *Markings* (New York: Alfred A. Knopf, 1964), p. 89.

STUDY GUIDE

for

Affirmative Aging:
a resource for ministry

for use by: individuals
study groups
Christian Education Committees
Social Action/Outreach groups
Pastoral Care Training
Parish Ministries
Episcopal Church Women
Housing Administrators

EPISCOPAL SOCIETY FOR MINISTRY ON AGING, INC.

ABOUT THE BOOK AND THE STUDY GUIDE

AFFIRMATIVE AGING is a book for clergy and laity, for individuals and groups, committees, task forces and study groups—both Episcopal and interfaith. It is for those committed to a ministry for and by older persons, and interested in the spiritual potential of our later years. Clergy and lay leaders will undoubtedly be the prime source of encouragement for the use of the book and study guide in their congregations.

This is not a book simply to be read and reflected upon. It is meant to challenge individuals and congregations to private and corporate action.

The book is a tool. It invites readers to consider the variety of ways in which life-styles, environments, and attitudes affect the developing spiritual life of our later years. The Study Guide provides formats for exploring the basic issues of each chapter. There are also suggestions given for individual self-study beginning on page 181.

SUGGESTIONS FOR USE.

Christian Education Groups.

Group Study for better understanding of the educational needs of older persons.

Resource materials for programs and classes for older adults.

Social Action/Outreach Groups.

Group study to consider how environments and activities affect spiritual well-being.

For special use in nursing home ministries and with other programs for the frail elderly.

Pastoral Care Groups.

A **must** for volunteers and other personnel, especially the chapters on spiritual development and death preparation.

Pastoral Concerns Groups.

Program resources for groups such as: adult children/aging parents; aging parents/adult children; support groups for care-givers of frail elders.

AGING, A SPIRITUAL JOURNEY
T. Herbert O'Driscoll

Purpose: To present an opportunity for an assessment of one's perspective on the nature of spirituality and life.

Note: **It is imperative for all participants to read the chapter prior to the session.**

STEP 1: Divide into small groups. A minimum of four is necessary. Assign each group one of the following statements or questions. Using the book, list ways the author understands spirituality as it relates to the assigned statement.

    1. How has "it" been known to the author?
    2. What changes in society and the church have affected present spirituality?
    3. Our Faith story is more than past event—it is also present reality.
    4. Christ is not just a personal Savior, but Lord and Judge of institutions.

STEP 2: Reconvene and invite each group to share its findings.

STEP 3: Silent Reflection.
What responses from your own spiritual life can you make to the four statements? What aspects of your life in the Christian community have been helpful?

STEP 4: Divide the group into pairs of younger and older partners to share Step 3 insights. Look for similarities and differences. Is age a factor? Why? why not?

STEP 5: Reconvene and allow time for sharing any general observations and feelings and/or learnings about the chapter.

TOWARD AN ETHIC FOR THE THIRD AGE
Charles J. Fahey

Purpose: To consider life as a journey with common challenges of growth and change. To use this concept as a beginning exploration into an understanding and preparation for the Third Age.

STEP 1: Leader preparation: Divide a large sheet of newsprint or shelf paper into three parts. At the far left corner make a large dot. Label it "BIRTH".

Involve the group in creating the "Life-Map" or "Trip-Tik." Draw a roadway along which significant events are labeled, using Fahey's concepts of the three ages. Encourage topological indications such as winding roads, mountains, rivers, deserts, and landmark beginnings such as "walk," "speech," "first date," etc.

Stop at the Third Age.

Divide into small groups to discuss:

"Will the road now go up or down?"
"Why? Why not?"
"What will help or hinder the journey?"
"What will the landmarks be?"

Reconvene to share ideas. Complete the map.

STEP 2: Return to small groups and using Fahey's chapter discuss:

"In what ways could the church support our journey through the Third Age?"

Reconvene and share ideas.

STEP 3: Discuss in the total group:

"In what ways do you think our congregation is now doing some of these things? Could more be done? What? How?"

CHALLENGE TO MINISTRY: OPPORTUNITIES FOR THE OLDER PERSON
Emma Lou Benignus

Purpose: To help participants identify those longings important to the growth and development of spirituality in older persons, to empathize with them, and to move toward attitudes which will help parishes plan and work toward the empowerment of older persons.

STEP 1: Ask group members to skim the chapter to refresh their memories and to choose one illustration which excites them or with which they can identify.

STEP 2: In small or total group(s) invite each participant to share his/her choice and tell why it is a model. At what point does it speak to hopes and wishes for future development?

STEP 3: The author suggests that our older years are a new age with a new spiritual potential. Discuss these questions:

"Considering the story you have chosen what are some of the characteristics you see of the new age?"

"What are some of the stumbling blocks we can identify in society and the church which could hinder and block the movement of older persons into the new age?"

"What transformations in our parish life and environment would make it more possible for older persons to manifest the wishes and visions of the new age?"

STEP 4: Consider writing, individually or as a group, a rite of passage for the movement from the time of employment to the years of "retirement," or from the "active household" to the "empty nest."

MEDITATION AND PRAYER
Nancy Roth

Purpose: To identify difficulties in past prayer disciplines, to experience one of the models given in the chapter, and to encourage further exploration at home. (2 Sessions.)

Prayer is the heart and life-blood of spiritual development. The ultimate goal of corporate worship and a disciplined prayer life is the gradual unfolding of a relationship between the person and God. Many models for disciplined prayer have evolved from experience. This chapter offers three models which have proved useful over time.

STEP 1: Ask each person to list two or three difficulties experienced in private prayer life.

STEP 2: Post the following questions. In small groups discuss the participants' impressions of the chapter.

"What ideas excited you? seemed appropriate? were new? made you uncomfortable? Were there any models you have tried and rejected? Does any model seem to offer a way out of previous difficulties?"

STEP 3: **Prepare two or three assistants to help you with this step.** Each leader will be responsible for conducting a portion of one of the three models given in the chapter. Each participant will elect one model to experience.

Homework: Encourage participants to continue using the chosen model in the coming week. Invite them to return the following week to share reactions and learnings.

STEP 4: Report back and discuss the following questions.

"Was the experience what you hoped for?"
"What changes would you make? Additions?"
"What next steps would you take?"
"What further helps would be useful?"

THE GIFT OF WISDOM
Robert W. Carlson

Purpose: To identify the characteristics of wisdom, and reflect on their development in order to help persons understand the potential for a unique wisdom achieved by embracing the challenges of old age.

STEP 1: Provide participants with paper and pencil. Ask them to think of a person of any age whom they consider to be wise, and to reflect on this question:

"What characteristics or qualities lead you to the opinion that they are wise?"

Share ideas and then discuss the following:

"Which of these qualities would be in **your** definition of wisdom? Why?"

STEP 2: Divide into small groups to discuss the following questions and ideas.

The author suggests that wisdom comes from a "honing" of life. Looking back over your life, what experiences have helped you see life in perspective or wholeness? If wisdom is fundamentally a gift of God, in what ways do you accept or reject **your** aging as God's gift? How does this idea balance with the desire to "own your life?"

STEP 4: Individual Exercise: Write a paragraph or poem expressing your idea about life's wholeness. These need not be signed, but individuals might share, or they could be read by the leader. Discuss these questions:

"Are there common threads or themes which run through all of them? Are there differences or uniquenesses? Do any make a difference in the interpretation of your experiences? How do they correlate with your listing of the characteristics and qualities of wisdom?"

INTERGENERATIONAL RELATIONSHIPS: ADULT CHILDREN AND AGING PARENTS
Helen Kandel Hyman

Purpose: To help participants express feelings relating to their own experience of the phenomenon of multi-generational living with its attendant joys and sorrows, and to explore some of the options available in their situation, freeing them to live with the issues.

STEP 1: Divide into small groups of five or six. Each person should have a copy of the following "Beatitudes." Allow time for ample sharing of personal feelings.

BEATITUDES ON AGING.
Blessed are those:
...who perform their care-giver's role without feelings of inadequacy or guilt. (Not caring for those who cared for us.)
...whose families are the primary support system for elderly relatives.
...who do not juggle conflicting responsibilities as adult children—as adult children with elderly parents and adolescent children—as empty nesters bent on retirement—as retired children with elderly parents.
...who are elderly and moderately healthy, independent, controlling their own lives, financially "fixed", and sexually oriented.
...who accept the diversity of the aging process as it occurs in individuals.

Summarize feelings and ideas common to all.

STEP 2: Reconvene and share the summaries.
Discuss:

"What faith resources can help children and parents as they relate through the difficulties of the latter years?"

STEP 3: Either in the group or individually rewrite your own "Beatitudes."

THE CHURCH, AN INFORMAL SUPPORT FOR AGING

Claudia B. Cluff and Leighton E. Cluff

Purpose: To move toward more significant and intentional support by the church for the care-givers of the frail elderly, through reflection on the importance of giving and receiving human support in the care of the frail elderly.

STEP 1: Allow time for each participant to list brief responses to the following questions.

> "Given your experiences, what is your reaction to the author's perspective on the lack of informal support for the frail elderly and their care-givers?"
> "In your experience what are/were the difficulties?"
> "How are they different or similar to the author's?"

Share answers with the group. Discuss differences and similarities of answers.

STEP 2: Divide into small groups of five to eight. Consider the following quote from the author:

> "The provision of human support in caring for older persons is a substantial component of health care...enhancing the quality of an individual's life...But the intermittent intervention of professionals cannot satisfactorily replace the human support of family, friends, neighbors or religious communities. Samaritism and technology are the cornerstone of medical practice."

> "How could your church realistically address the need for human support...for church members...for those in the wider community?"
> "What would a model for action look like?"
> "What realities would you need to take into account?"
> "What first steps would be taken?"

Report to the total group.

STEP 3: Discuss plans for similarities and differences. Evaluate those which could begin immediately and those requiring more time and preparation. Decide on first steps. Assign responsibilities. Plan for a follow-up session to begin setting goals and putting plans into action.

LEISURE AND LEARNING: A SPIRITUAL PERSPECTIVE

Nancy J. Osgood

Purpose: To explore and consider changes or improvements in the theory and practice of leisure for yourself and others.

STEP 1: Supply 5×8 cards and pencils. Ask each participant to write down three ways in which they spend their leisure time and sign their name.

STEP 2: Post all the cards on a bulletin board or other similar surface. Ask participants to "shop" for a card with leisure activities different from their own. Find the owner and dialogue briefly about the reasons for the choices. If there is time, repeat this step.

STEP 3: Gather the group and discuss the following:

"Based on your conversations what would you list as the characteristics or criteria of a satisfactory leisure experience?"

STEP 4: Using the book ask the group to prepare a list of criteria given by the author, or have this list prepared in advance. Compare the author's list with the group's list for similarities and differences.

STEP 5: Invite individual responses to the following:

"Based on the discussion what changes would you consider in your approach to leisure time and activities?"

STEP 6: If your church or organization offers leisure time activities for the elderly how do they fit the author's criteria?
What unique opportunities might the church provide?

STEP 7: Develop a model for your church or organization, taking into account the realities of your local situation. What is the first step?

CREATIVE LIVING ENVIRONMENTS FOR OLDER PERSONS

Charles W. Pruitt, Jr.

Purpose: To reflect on the way past living environments affected one's quality of life, as a motivation for change in existing stereo-typical living environments and to encourage church and community involvement in future planning.

STEP 1: Ask each participant to reflect on and write down memories in response to the following: Think of the home you most enjoyed living in. What did you like about it? How did it make you feel? What effect did living there have on your self-image? your relationships?

Think of the same questions for the home you liked least.

What does your perspective on these two experiences suggest to you about the living arrangements you will need in the next thirty years to insure a positive impact on your life style, dignity and life satisfaction?

Divide into small groups and share some of your findings. What similarities and differences are apparent?

STEP 2: In small groups discuss the following:
How has this made you feel about your present living environment? Future? What does this suggest about the stereotyping that occurs in planning housing for older persons?

STEP 3: List the various housing alternatives suggested in the chapter. Given the realities of human and financial resources in your parish and/or community, what could your parish do to create new housing or improve aspects of existing residential living for the elderly? Does a potential exist for working ecumenically?

What first steps could you or your group take?

DEATH PREPARATION AS LIFE ENHANCEMENT
Eugene C. Bianchi

Purpose: To help persons affirm their past in order to plan, enhance and accept their future in the light of their own mortality.

STEP 1: Give each person a magazine: (*Time, Newsweek,* etc.). Ask each one to find five or six pictures or words which have significance for... "who you are today, your values, attitudes, concerns, causes, desires in terms of legacy, important acquisitions in your environment, etc. Include hobbies, activities, if these are an important part." If appropriate pictures and words cannot be found, encourage writing the desired words.

STEP 2: Each person is to choose a partner with whom to share his/her story. (If possible match a younger person with an older person.) Tell why pictures were chosen and what they symbolize.

Identify those which symbolize long term interests and ideas and those related to recent developments. How are they different from each other? In what ways, if any, did a sense of one's mortality precipitate possible changes in attitudes, and values. Do these changes enhance life or are they potentially negative influences?

STEP 3: Reconvene. Provide an opportunity for sharing, but do not labor or force this.

STEP 4: (Could be a group or individual activity.) Provide each person with a notebook or suggest this as a later follow-up. Suggest that the words and pictures be pasted into the notebook. Encourage adding new thoughts, creation of a litany of thanksgiving, a bequest to someone—tangible or intangible, a statement of hope for the future. If a group litany is written use it as a prayer or meditation in closing or at a Eucharist.

STUDY SUGGESTIONS FOR INDIVIDUALS

You may find it helpful to keep a notebook in which you will write the responses to the exercises. This could be the beginning of a journal you will continue after reading the book.

When numbered steps are mentioned, they indicate an exercise in the previous group formats.

Chapter 1. Aging, A Spiritual Journey.

Outline the chapter using the categories under Step 1. Try repeating the exercise based on your own experience. How is your experience similar or different from the author's? Is age a factor? How are you experiencing "it" in your life currently? What ideas do you have for becoming more intentional about growth in this aspect of your life?

Chapter 2. Toward an Ethic for the Third Age.

Create a Life-Map using the book and the instructions from Step 1. Reflect on your work and write a paragraph stating your hopes for your Third Age. What preparations are you making now or how are you now living in this age? What help do you need? Where can you find it? You may find it helpful to discuss your thoughts with another lay person or your clergy person.

Chapter 3. Challenge to Ministry: Opportunities for the Older Person.

Follow Steps 1, 2, 3, 4, and 6 in the group format. Use the questions to help you develop new avenues for your own spiritual growth.

Chapter 4. Meditation and Prayer.

List some difficulties or stumbling blocks in your prayer life. Select a model from the chapter and integrate it into your contemplative life for a short period. Reflect on your experience and write out your reactions, i.e. was it what you hoped for? Was it helpful? Why? Why not? Repeat with the other models. You may want to share your experience with another parish member, or clergy person.

Chapter 5. The Gift of Wisdom.

Select an older person who is a model for you. Reflect on the qualities you most admire. Do you think they have the gift of wisdom? Why? Using Step 2 think about your role model and yourself. Write a paragraph about your sense of wholeness or lack of it in your life.

Chapter 6. Intergenerational Relationships.

Look at the "Beatitudes on Aging" under Step 1. Reflect on your own feelings as you read them. Try writing "Beatitudes" of your own.

Chapter 7. The Church, An Informal Support for Aging.

Think about the questions in Step 1. In what ways can you improve or change your situation? Do you know where to find resources for help? Explore your phone book for information about services for older persons. Could you become a support person for a frail elder and his/her family?

Chapter 8. Leisure and Learning.

Make your own list of the ways you spend your leisure time. List **your** criteria for making your choices. How is it similar or different from the author's? What changes in your use of leisure would you consider, if any?

Chapter 9. Creative Living Environments for Older Persons.

Using the chapter as your resource, what new living environment options are open to you or someone you know? How does it effect your "feelings" about your future planning? Could you be more involved in the planning for older adult housing in your community?

Chapter 10. Death Preparation as Life Enhancement.

Use Step 1 and reflect on what your pictures suggest about changes in attitudes and feelings from the past to the present. How does the sense of your mortality bear on these changes, if it does? Try the suggestion in Step 4. Add pictures and writing to your notebook.

The Study Guide © was Prepared for

by
Julie Armstrong
Frances Reynolds Johnson

The Study Guide was made possible by a grant from the Social Welfare Office of the Episcopal Church Center.

Below is bibliographical information for the references in "Leisure and Learning: A Spiritual Perspective" by Nancy J. Osgood. U.S. Bureau of the Census, 1981: U.S. Senate Special Committee on Aging. *Developments in Aging: 1980, Part I*. Washington: Government Printing Office.

Buhler, C. "Meaningful Living in the Mature Years." *In Aging and Leisure, A Research Perspective*, ed. R. Kleemier. New York: Oxford University Press, 1961.

Cox, Harvey. *The Feast of Fools*. New York: Harper & Row, 1967.

Dahl, G. *Work, Play, and Worship*. Minneapolis: Augsburg Publishing House, 1972.

Dangott, L. R. and R. A. Kalish. *A Time to Enjoy the Pleasures of Aging*. Englewood Cliffs, NJ: Prentice-Hall, 1979.

Gross, R., B. Gross, and S. Seidman, eds. *The New Old: Struggling for Decent Aging*. Garden City, NY: Doubleday, 1978.

Kelly, J. R. *Leisure*. Englewood Cliffs, NJ: Prentice-Hall, 1982.

Keen, Sam. *To a Dancing God*. New York: Harper & Row, 1970.

Lee, R. "From Holy Days to Holidays." *Phi Kappa Phi* (1964) 62: 29-31.

Mobley, T. A. "Leisure Counseling: A New Profession." Phi Kappa Phi (1982) 62: 16-17.

Moltmann, Jürgen. *Theology of Play*. New York: Harper & Row, 1972.

Pieper, Josef. *Leisure: The Basis of Culture*, trans. Alexander Dru. New York: Pantheon Books, 1952.

Tilgher, A. *Work: What It Has Meant to Men Through the Ages*, trans. D. Fischer. New York: Harcourt Brace, 1930.

Underhill, Evelyn. *Worship*. New York: Harper & Row, 1937.

The Episcopal Society for Ministry on Aging is a national resource for the Episcopal Church for developing ministries with and on behalf of older persons. ESMA works through denominational, interfaith, and societal networks to serve the needs of spirit, mind, and body of the aging and promotes their continued contribution to church and society, maximizing their unique gifts and talents.

The Episcopal Society for Ministry on Aging
R.D. 4, Box 146A
Milford, New Jersey 08848
Phone: (201) 995-2885

Additional copies of *Affirmative Aging* may be obtained from the ESMA office.